...gsburg College
George Sverdrup Library
Minneapolis, Minnesota 55404

D0984034

Shaking the Money Tree

Shaking

HOW TO FIND NEW GROWTH OPPORTUNITIES

the Money Tree

IN COMMON STOCKS

Winthrop Knowlton AND John L. Furth

HARPER & ROW, PUBLISHERS

NEW YORK, EVANSTON, SAN FRANCISCO, LONDON

1817

Portions of this book previously appeared in *Growth Opportunities in Common Stocks* by Winthrop Knowlton. Copyright © 1965 by Winthrop Knowlton. Published by Harper & Row, Publishers, Inc.

SHAKING THE MONEY TREE: HOW TO FIND NEW GROWTH OPPORTUNITIES IN COMMON STOCKS. *Copyright © 1972 by Winthrop Knowlton and John L. Furth. All rights reserved. Printed in the United States of America. No part of this book may be used or reproduced in any manner whatsoever without written permission except in the case of brief quotations embodied in critical articles and reviews. For information address Harper & Row, Publishers, Inc., 10 East 53rd Street, New York, N.Y. 10022. Published simultaneously in Canada by Fitzhenry & Whiteside Limited, Toronto.*

FIRST EDITION

LIBRARY OF CONGRESS CATALOG CARD NUMBER: 76-156529

STANDARD BOOK NUMBER: 06-012441-5

HG
4521
K57

To Grace and Hope

1 2 0 8 0 5

Contents

viii | *Contents*

Acknowledgments

The authors are indebted to Thomas P. Larsen for his assistance in the preparation of the financial data, including the tables, used in this book. They are also indebted to Lucia Withers, Beth Tracy, E. Terri Herman, Kaethie Saxon, and Christa M. Janssens for their help in various aspects of manuscript preparation. Other useful advice and assistance has been provided by Thomas C. Pryor, Frank Ritger, and Peter Strauss, who took the time to read a number of chapters in their earlier stages. Last but not least we are grateful to Virginia Hilu, Richard E. Passmore and Lesley Krauss for their editorial assistance at Harper & Row.

"What is more mortifying than to
feel that you've missed the plum for want
of courage to shake the tree?"
                    LOGAN PEARSALL SMITH

Introduction

Wʜᴀᴛ ɪs ᴀ ᴍᴏɴᴇʏ ᴛʀᴇᴇ?

IBM is a money tree, a great corporation that put its roots down many years ago, started growing and branching out, and has been doing so ever since. We are taught that trees do not grow to the sky. But to the early investor who put $5,000 into the stock of this company twenty years ago and who today has $286,814, the top of this tree is close enough.

Avon Products and Xerox* are money trees, too—firmly established, successful companies that continue to branch out, to grow consistently, each year, every year. These are the kinds of money trees investors have been able to hang onto in the last two decades and to shake, with pleasant results.

What will be the great money trees of the next ten years? Are IBM, Avon, and Xerox still the fastest-growing, the most promising investments? How can you tell?

The purpose of this book is to help show you how to tell and, in so doing, to help you make a fair return on your investment in the stock market.

* A $5,000 investment in Avon Products in 1950 has grown to $2.3 million today; the same investment in Xerox (then the Haloid Company) would be worth $2.9 million. All figures exclude dividends received during the period.

This is *not* a muckraking book. It is *not* a book about how the man in the street has been led down the garden path by the men of Wall Street in the last few years. There are plenty of other books around describing Wall Street as a jungle or a sheep pen in which you, the individual buyer of securities, are repeatedly fleeced. If you're a glutton (or mutton) for punishment, read one of those.

Why have individual investors found it so difficult to make attractive returns in the stock market in recent years? We believe there are four major problems:

- Lack of reasonable objectives. Typically, the investor reaches for too high a return too fast. He's unrealistic and impatient. So are his advisers. These are human failings.
- Lack of a clear-cut investment philosophy. What kinds of companies does the investor want to own and why?
- Lack of sophistication in selecting individual investments. He doesn't really understand the key ingredients that make for enduring corporate success or those that cause corporate failure. He doesn't recognize a money tree when he sees one; often he sees one that isn't there.
- Lack of an investment strategy that permits him to put his objectives, his philosophy, and his selections effectively together in a strong portfolio of common stocks. To do this he needs to know how to find and use professional investment advice; how to time his purchases and sales; and how interest rates and bond prices influence his common stock commitments.

This book addresses itself to these four problems: objectives (Chapter 2); philosophy (Chapter 3); selection (Chapters 4–10); and implementation (Chapters 11–13). The heart of the book, in the authors' judgment, is the section on *selection,* in which we attempt to help the reader understand what makes certain companies go forward and others sputter and stall. How can you tell when a successful company is changing—when the tree is growing old, or becoming vulnerable to blight, or about to topple in a competitive storm it once could have weathered? How can you tell when a small, specialized company (like Xerox in 1960) has the potential to move dramatically ahead?

The four sections of the book described above are bracketed by an opening chapter that describes the turbulent events of the period 1965–1971—seven years that left many investors bruised and battered—and a concluding chapter that is foolish enough to speculate on a few problems and opportunities that lie ahead of us in the 1970s.

Writing a book on the stock market is always a perilous, and usually a presumptuous, undertaking. The authors of this book have logged, collectively, twenty-seven years on Wall Street and seven years outside Wall Street with the federal government and industry. We have called on, and studied, thousands of corporations in our days as security analysts. We have managed investment portfolios. Today one of us is helping to manage a privately owned investment-counseling and venture-capital firm; the other is helping to manage a publicly owned publishing house. (Today, somewhat to our surprise, security analysts call on us!)

If this background does not qualify us, then perhaps our mistakes do. We have made plenty of them. We have bought overpriced growth stocks that were about to fall apart at the seams, and we have bought undervalued problem companies that remained undervalued or that didn't solve their problems. And then there were the companies we sold . . . the really good ones that got away. . . . We think we've learned from these mistakes (as well as from a few successes, here and there). We hope this book—if it does nothing else—prevents you from making the same errors. Absence of the "big goof" does wonders for one's overall investment performance.

Our enthusiasm for the successful companies we describe in this book may seem callous to some readers in view of the extraordinary social problems created in this country by mindless corporate growth. We believe that the answer to many of these problems lies not in zero growth but in *intelligent, planned direction.* Perhaps the leaders of a few of the companies in question will be instrumental in helping provide such direction.

We believe there will be further economic growth in the trillion-dollar American economy and in the two-trillion-dollar economy of the industrialized world. In such a world we believe there will be ways for investors to earn rewarding returns from carefully selected common stocks—no matter how troublesome the present or unpredictable the future.

This book attempts to help them find the best way.

January, 1972

Shaking the Money Tree

1

Looking Back

Aт the beginning of 1965 Lyndon B. Johnson had just been re-elected President of the United States, pledging no wider war.

The economy was moving along nicely, its prospects enhanced by recent passage of the most stimulative tax reduction program in the modern economic history of the country. The economic recovery of the first half of the decade had been virtually inflation free—such inflation averaging only 1.3 percent per annum during the period 1960–1964.*

The federal government's ability to effect social change appeared improved as a result not only of President Johnson's early legislative accomplishments but also of the substantially larger Congressional majority won by his party in the 1964 election.

The corporate community, if not euphoric, was self-confident. Corporate after-tax profits had improved from $26.7 billion in 1960 to $38.4 billion in 1964. A number of individual corporations had been making extraordinary progress in opening up vast new markets—IBM, Avon, and Xerox among them. These companies appeared to be in control of their destinies, generating

* Inflation throughout this book is measured by the Consumer Price Index. Readers may be startled at the realization that President Kennedy launched his 1962 attack on steel price increases in as mild an inflationary setting as that described above.

1

products for which there were powerful new demands (in fact, investments in these companies subsequently worked out well, despite the mostly unpleasant surprises of the late sixties).

Corporate managements and the investment community were gradually persuading themselves that technology, new marketing skills, and modern management techniques could indeed be harnessed in exciting new ways; that new products and market needs could be "engineered"; and that virtually irrevocable increases in sales and earnings would thus come about. (Not long thereafter the distinguished French journalist J. J. Servan-Schreiber confirmed this pleasurable appraisal of American managerial expertise in his widely read book, *The American Challenge.**)

Operating in a favorable political and economic environment, making loads of money itself, the Wall Street community was in no mood then, and for several years thereafter, to question very deeply or for very long the clouds that began to gather on the horizon. It looked forward to continuing, rising, tranquil prosperity.

In fact, we were entering one of the most turbulent periods in the history of our nation. This turbulence was soon to be reflected in the behavior of all our securities markets.

Starting at 874.13 on December 31, 1964, the Dow Jones Industrial Average reached an all-time high of 995.15 in 1966. It exceeded 900 in 1967, 1968, and 1969, but by May 1970 it had plummeted to 631 (the lowest figure since 1962), wiping out not only years of statistical progress but also the careers, reputations, and fortunes created through such presumed progress. Since May 1970 the market has recovered, in fits and starts, but as of this writing (December 1971) it is only slightly higher than it was seven years ago.† The recovery of the economy and the stock market has been an erratic affair.

---

* New York: Atheneum Publishers, 1968. Executives might better have heeded Somerset Maugham's earlier description of "American Delusions: (1) that there is no class-consciousness in the country; (2) that American coffee is good; (3) that Americans are business-like; (4) that Americans are highly sexed and that redheads are more highly sexed than others."

† The Standard & Poor's 500 reached an all-time high of 108.37 in November 1968. This average had recovered to 102.93 at the end of 1971 from a low of 69.29 in May 1970.

Interest rates moved inexorably higher during the period 1965–1970, as illustrated in the table on page 4.

There was an almost chaotic churning of securities. In 1964 daily trading in common stocks listed on the New York Stock Exchange averaged only 4.9 million shares. On the busiest day that year, 6.9 million shares changed hands. By 1968 *average* daily trading had climbed to 13 million shares. One day that year the figure reached a high of 21.3 million shares, a daily volume total that became common by 1971.

What caused the turbulence of the late sixties and the market convulsion of early 1970? What has happened since? What are the implications of these events for investors? Could and did some investors do better than the market? What lessons can we learn? What lessons, *if any,* have Wall Street and its clientele learned? These questions will come up repeatedly in this book as we attempt to approach the problem of investing in American corporations with due but not excessive regard for the lessons of recent history.

In retrospect, causes of economic and market upheaval in the second half of the sixties are not hard to come by:

- As the economic recovery progressed, inflation increased. In 1965 the rate moved up from the aforementioned (1960–1964) figure of 1.3 percent to 1.5 percent.
- Normal inflationary pressures were exacerbated in the following years by the Vietnam war, by an ambitious domestic social welfare program, and by the failure of government officials to grasp fully or to respond adequately to their economic impact.
- The business community responded to the powerful combination of continuing real economic growth, mounting inflation, and administration commitments to "guns and butter" by going on a speculative rampage. Corporations launched ambitious capital-spending programs. They worked hard to construct new enterprises ("conglomerates") comprised of disparate, loosely connected commercial entities that were magically expected, in the hands of facile, self-confident managements, to "synergize."

These corporate acquisitions and mergers were financed through the use of fixed-income securities (long- and short-term debt and preferred stocks) and heavy bank borrowings, as well as common stock.

- Consumers increased spending, too, using a host of credit devices to do so.
- Investors of all kinds, individual and institutional, domestic and foreign, bought common stocks, adding to the demands for credit.
- With the exception of several short-lived flurries, bond prices fell and interest rates rose to historic heights not seen since the Civil War. (See the table below.)

Interest Rates on Selected Fixed-Income Securities

	1970	1969	1968	1967	1966	1965
91-day Treasury bills	6.42%	6.64%	5.33%	4.30%	4.85%	3.95%
3–5 year Treasury notes	7.37	6.85	5.59	5.07	5.16	4.22
Moody's corporate AAA bonds	8.04	7.03	6.18	5.51	5.13	4.49
Moody's long-term* state and local AAA bonds	6.12	5.45	4.20	3.74	3.67	3.16

Source: Federal Reserve Bulletin, *February 1971. Averages for the year.*
* Maturing or callable in 10 years or more.

During 1969 inflation reached an annual rate of 5.4 percent. As Sydney Homer, partner-scholar of Salomon Brothers, wrote: "It was the first inflation in the history of this country that came to be accepted as a way of life."

Meanwhile, the social and political stability upon which orderly (let alone climbing) securities markets ultimately depend was deteriorating.

Again Vietnam was the fuse—setting off an explosion of national dissatisfaction with issues long dormant but now freshly perceived. Racial inequity, poverty, erosion of the quality of our civil liberties and of our environment—these were specific subjects of concern, bringing violence to our cities and our campuses, adding stress to the relationship between generations and classes, and creating widespread lack of self-confidence about two issues fundamental to all others: our ability to order our national priorities and, having done so, to effect peaceful change.

War, inflation, and speculation interacted, bloating stock prices during 1967 and 1968.

Coupled with, and somewhat confused by, belated federal measures (tax increases and tightened money supply) to *curb* inflation, the same factors interacted again in 1969 and 1970 to help produce high interest rates, a reduction in real economic growth, the social unrest just described, political uncertainty, and the sharpest stock market reversal of the postwar period. Early reactions to inflation—the first realizations that it was becoming "a way of life"—induced near-panic purchasing (or so it seems today) of American equities in 1967 and 1968 by foreign as well as domestic investors. The opposite reaction set in late in 1969 and early in 1970. Cambodia, Kent State, and Penn Central brought the decline in confidence and values to crisis proportions in the spring of the latter year.

Let us turn from consideration of these broad economic, social, and political forces to the internal dynamics of the financial community itself. Structural and attitudinal changes in Wall Street took place, in part, as a result of the external forces we have described. At the same time the Street's practices, values, and moods exerted their own influence on securities markets. On balance these were not beneficial forces—either for those investing as individuals or for those utilizing institutional intermediaries such as pension or mutual funds.

In a later chapter we discuss the increasing institutionalization of the American stock market during this period and the implications of this for you, the individual investor. Suffice it to say here that, between the beginning and the end of the decade, purchases (or sales) of equities on the New York Stock Exchange by individuals declined from 69 to 45 percent of all transactions.* Transactions by "institutional" clients—pension funds, insurance companies, mutual funds, etc.—increased proportionately. To some

Net Share Purchases and Net New Issues of Corporate Shares

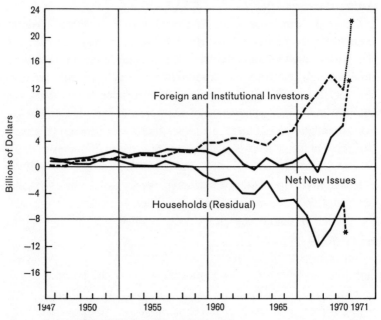

Source: Federal Reserve Flow of Funds
*Preliminary 1971 first half at annual rate.

extent Wall Street turned its back on individual investors, preferring to direct its energies, attention, and talents to the large institutional intermediaries—representing individuals, to be sure—whom it was more lucrative to serve. To some extent the individual investor turned his back on the stock market, too. The chart above illustrates the extent of this dramatic shift.

* *New York Stock Exchange 1970 Fact Book,* p. 50.

Abetting this process of "institutionalization," and playing a critical role in the investment community in this difficult period, was a new breed of money manager: Adam Smith's "gunslingers."*

The gunslingers developed self-confidence early in their careers. Often with graduate-business-school backgrounds, sometimes with industrial or marketing experience outside Wall Street, they moved into the financial community and, benefiting from the ability to pick stocks effectively in the early stages of a bull market, moved quickly into positions of responsibility as analysts, salesmen, or portfolio managers. Like their more cerebral counterparts in the Pentagon, they prided themselves on their charts, their analytical skills, their quickness of judgment, their decision-making abilities. Speed in recognizing new corporate products, services, or markets; speed in analyzing the impact of complex mergers; speed in digesting information fed from other analysts; speed in moving in and out of securities—as deftly as Roger Staubach slips out of "the pocket" and throws to an open receiver—became ends in themselves.

The need to obtain information, and to act upon it quickly, was important because portfolio managers found themselves caught up in a race of their own making in which superior *short-range* investment performance paid off—by attracting more investors to the better-performing funds. More investors meant more money for these funds to manage, higher management fees, higher salaries for portfolio managers, and more commissions for the brokers and investment bankers who helped ensure the superior financial performance. In a sense (and for a while) the performance *was* ensured for the quicker-moving funds because other, slower-moving institutional purchasers, gradually caught up in the emotions of a speculative market, attempted to emulate the better performers by purchasing the "hot" stocks in their more nimble competitors' portfolios, thus driving the issues in question up still further.

* Lewis Lapham of *Harper's Magazine* has described them, less charitably, as "wise-ass kids." See 'Adam Smith,' *The Money Game,* New York: Random House, 1968.

This process—not unlike that preceding the 1929 crash—helped account for the immense amount of institutional trading in securities, for the tremendous volume of trading, for the volatility of individual stocks and, ultimately, for that of the market as a whole.

Just as certain forces in the larger economic, political, and social spheres interacted to move history along a particular course, so these attitudes and values in the corporate world, in the Wall Street world of brokers and investment bankers, and in the burgeoning world of institutional investment management, coalesced, reinforced one another, and moved the stock market first up and then down a tumultuous path in the late sixties.

Corporate executives, assisted by staffs of merger and acquisition experts and under immense pressure from the financial community to provide flawless earnings growth from quarter to quarter and year to year, lacked the patience and the courage required for slow, solid, even if occasionally erratic, internal growth. Growth through acquisition tended to become the rule. The larger the scale, the more complex the financial technique, and the more abrupt the transformation of the concern's image, the more the market applauded.

Investment bankers abetted this process, in their hunger for fees earned from helping to negotiate mergers and the "spreads" earned from floating new security issues.

Security analysts no longer studied industries in depth or allowed the irreplaceable ingredient of time to season their judgments. They depended increasingly on the telephone, calling institutional clients immediately after talking to corporate presidents or financial officers. In the scramble for institutional commissions, it was important for analysts to be "visible" to institutional buyers and sellers, and to "communicate" the latest information, usually educated guesses about forthcoming *quarterly* earnings performance. Research analysts became large producers of commission business for their firms. Corporations anxious to be recognized as companies that were of "institutional" quality—with their shares prominently displayed in institutional portfolios—helped play the game, providing information and becoming still more aggressive in acquisition and promotional activities.

And so it went. The idea that great business enterprises are made—made over lifetimes of hard managerial effort—and not born in the minds of security analysts or portfolio managers went out of style. Distinctions between investment and speculation were lost. Fiduciary responsibilities were not met.

The description is, of course, oversimplified and overdramatized. Many companies, many Wall Street firms, many individual analysts, and many institutional buyers resisted the temptations described, but they represented a smaller portion of the total financial community as the decade progressed. An industry that prided itself on its analytical skills in appraising management and corporate fortunes—this, really, is Wall Street's raison d'être—so mismanaged its own business that it was forced to close its own doors one day out of five to bring order out of the chaos of its internal affairs.* More than one hundred firms ultimately closed their doors for good or were absorbed by stronger houses. Thousands of employees lost jobs.

The period since the summer of 1970 has been calmer but by no means trouble free. The actions of the government, of corporations, and of the Wall Street community have in large measure been aimed at picking up the pieces of the year just described. Such actions include the President's efforts to wind down the Vietnam war; to arrest inflation, first through applications of conventional fiscal and monetary medicine and, more recently and dramatically, through the unprecedented imposition of peacetime controls; and to restore international financial equilibrium by negotiating new foreign exchange rates. With few exceptions corporations have abandoned their "conglomerate" binges and have been working to cut costs and restore liquidity. Somewhat chastened, Wall Street

---

* The New York Stock Exchange suspended trading in securities, closed its business down, in effect, every Wednesday from June 12 to December 31, 1968, to enable itself and its member firms to catch up with their unprocessed backlog of business.

firms are attempting to manage themselves more rationally, and the Street talks and writes of reform.

The individual investor remains skeptical, continuing to sell stocks and buy bonds. Fears about inflation and unemployment linger. Will we be able to resolve international financial difficulties, or are we about to plunge into new, destructive forms of protectionism? Will corporate and economic growth of the sort to which we have been accustomed in the postwar period be possible or even tolerable in the decades ahead? We continue to substitute new uncertainties for old. What lessons can be learned from all this?

The first lesson, clearly, is that investors cannot take environmental stability for granted. In retrospect, the five-year period from 1960 to 1964 was unusually calm. Perhaps it seems more so now than it did then because of the subsequent turmoil and the distance of passing years. After all, we did have the Bay of Pigs, the Cuban missile crisis, Vietnam (on a much smaller scale), and a presidential assassination during those earlier years; however, the *economic* environment, characterized by relatively steady, broad, and inflation-free recovery, was comparatively placid. The political and social crises seemed isolated and sporadic rather than part of a disturbed continuum. While we do not foresee a continuation of the turbulent and violent environment of the late sixties, neither do we expect a return to the relatively arcadian preceding years.

Second: It is a mistake to underestimate the ease with which the Wall Street community can be swept up by the euphoria and/or paranoia of the "outside" world. Enthusiasm and fear are emotions easily and rapidly transmitted, and investment intermediaries intensify these emotions, rarely defuse or deflect them.

Third: Do not assume that *institutional* advisers are less prone to investment "fashions" than anyone else. They are human beings like the rest of us. As a corollary, do not take it for granted that a company is necessarily an attractive long-term holding because you find it listed in the portfolio of large mutual funds. "Dirt glitters," the saying goes, "when the sun happens to shine."

Fourth: The stock market has become, and is likely to remain, more sensitive to the level of interest rates than it was in the first two decades after World War II. As an individual investor you must be more alert to fixed-income securities as possible alternatives, from time to time, to common stocks.

Fifth: Don't put *all* your excess cash, ever, into the stock market. Accidents can happen.

Sixth: In selecting a broker (see Chapter 11), you must take increasing care to determine his ability and his desire to serve you as an individual client.

Finally, investment in quality companies has proved more rewarding—or, occasionally, less unrewarding—than investment in more speculative, erratic, less well-seasoned concerns. Selection of companies *with distinctive products and services catering to large and growing markets and in impeccable financial condition* was not always a foolproof approach to the stock market but it did provide surer and better returns than any other during the troubled times we have described.

OBJECTIVES

2

What Is a Reasonable Rate of Return?

You buy common stocks to make money. The table below indicates it has been difficult to do so lately.

You assume more risk when you buy a common stock than when you buy a preferred stock or a bond, or when you put your money into a savings account. You should receive a greater reward for doing so. No one can guarantee the reward, but if there are no rational grounds for believing the desired extra return is

Average Return* of Major Stock Exchange Indices

	12/31/64	12/31/70	12/31/71	Average Return 12/31/64 to 12/31/70	Average Return 12/31/64 to 12/31/71
Dow Jones Industrial Average	874.13	838.92	890.20	−0.7%	+0.2%
S & P 500 Composite Index	84.75	92.15	102.93	+1.4	+2.8
New York Stock Exchange Index	45.65	50.63	56.43	+1.6	+3.1

* Annual compounded rate.

15

possible, then clearly you should not put your money into common stocks.

The table on page 4 shows how much higher rates of return on competing fixed-income securities were in 1970 than in previous years. As interest rates skyrocketed in the late sixties, it became more difficult for common stocks to compete with these investment alternatives—and this proved to be one of the decisive factors in the collapse of stock prices in 1969 and 1970.

Today, sophisticated investors view common stocks as providing a total return from (1) anticipated earnings growth and (2) dividends. This is an increasingly modern concept. Initially, the dividend alone did the trick; then it was the dividend plus the growth rate; now this order has been inverted. The average dividend return for an industrial stock today amounts to between 3 and 4 percent, a bracket within which yield has been stabilized for the past ten years. If this were the total available return from equities, no one would buy them. As pointed out, the dramatic increase in interest rates in 1969 and 1970 created attractive alternative returns in high-grade long-term bonds.

Capital appreciation depends importantly, then, on (1) the ability of a company to increase its earnings and (2) the amount investors are willing to pay for the higher earnings. In 1970 the General Electric Company concluded a prolonged strike. Subsequently, in an unrelated move, it announced that it was selling its data-processing division, a part of its business that had been a drain on earnings for many years. In 1970 strike-depressed earnings were reported at 1.80 per share (adjusted for a 2-for-1 stock split in 1971), and the stock sold as low as 30 per share. Six months later, with the sale of the data-processing division to Honeywell concluded, and with earnings of approximately $2.60–$2.70 per share forecast for 1971, the same shares sold for 60, a gain of 100 percent in a year. The dividend averaged $1.30 per year over the period, or 4.3 percent on the original cost of the investment.

The amount by which corporate earnings increase over a period of years depends on the rate at which the economy as a whole is growing and the ability of individual corporations, because of innovational excellence and other factors, to match or exceed that rate. Among the "other factors" that have been important in recent years are managerial discipline—the ability to set priorities, *not* to attempt too much too quickly.

The amount investors are willing to pay for earnings (the price-earnings ratio) depends on the confidence with which they view the future. If they are optimistic about the outlook for a specific company or for general business, they may pay a great deal. In late 1961 the Dow Jones Industrial Average sold at over twenty-two times estimated 1961 earnings. Investors were obviously anticipating a meaningful improvement in earnings—and they were right. The earnings gain that took place during the next four years resulted from improved business conditions and lower federal income taxes. Not again during the decade did the marketplace have such high confidence in future earnings growth. In succeeding years the price-earnings ratio of the Dow Jones Industrial Average varied from a high of 19.1 times earnings in March 1964, to a low of slightly less than 13.0 times earnings in the panic-stricken bear market of the spring of 1970.

In the last five years corporate earnings as measured by the Dow Jones Industrial Average have fluctuated between $57.89 and $51.02 per share per year, the high recorded in 1968 and the low in 1970. Directionless earnings caused a gradual deterioration in price-earnings ratios between 1965 and 1970—from 18.3 times in 1965 to a range of 12.8–14.6 in 1970.* The importance of confidence, or a lack thereof, is demonstrated by this dramatic change. One can moralize indefinitely about what a "proper" price-earnings ratio is, but in the final analysis it depends as much on investors' glands as on their sense of propriety.

Yet many individual companies' earnings remained high, and even increased during these years.

What should your investment objectives be when you purchase

---

* The experience of the Standard & Poor's 500 Average closely parallels that of the Dow Jones Industrial Average during these years.

a common stock? How much can you reasonably expect to make, annually, from dividends and capital gains combined? As we point out a bit later, your expectations should not always be the same. You have to relate them to the alternatives available at the time. The rate of inflation is important, too. So is your tax rate.*

Today, we believe you should aim for a total annual return of 10 to 12 percent from your common stock investments.

In order for carefully chosen stocks to provide an overall return of 10 to 12 percent when they provide only 3 percent from dividends, you have to assume that: (1) corporate earnings will go up about 8 percent per year; (2) investors will pay at least the same amount for higher earnings, as they materialize, as they do today; or (3) in the event earnings growth and/or investor sentiment fall short of these goals, corporations will pay out a higher percentage of their earnings as dividends, and the annual return from *that* source will gradually move up, say, from 3 percent to 4 percent.†

Is an annual return of 10 to 12 percent in the realm of possibility? What are the major factors—positive and negative—likely to affect corporate earnings, investor attitudes, and hence market prices in the years ahead?

Among the positive arguments that can be marshaled to support the view that the outlook for earnings and equities is favorable are these:

1. Leaders of both political parties in the United States are profoundly influenced, when in office, by the Employment Act of 1946, which states:

---

* For the investor in a high income-tax bracket, common stocks must provide a higher return than for other investors because of the greater relative attractiveness of tax-free municipals.

† IBM is a case in point. IBM's dividend in 1971 amounted to $5.20 per share, compared with 60 cents per share ten years earlier. The 1971 dividend was *more than double* IBM's 1961 earnings.

The 4 percent limitation imposed on annual dividend increases by President Nixon's Committee on Dividends and Interest, a part of his Council on the Cost of Living, has temporarily altered this analysis of the role of dividends in providing a "total return."

It is the continuing policy and responsibility of the Federal Government to use all practicable means consistent with its needs and obligations . . . to utilize all its . . . resources for the purpose of creating and maintaining, in a manner calculated to foster and promote free competitive enterprise . . . conditions under which there will be afforded useful employment.

2. Leaders of both political parties have demonstrated their willingness to use a variety of methods to stimulate economic growth in the last decade—tax cuts, investment credits, and other incentives. President Nixon espouses such concepts as the "full-employment budget." Much Keynesian or "New" economics enjoys broad, bipartisan political support.

3. Economic growth will be sustained not only by the government, when necessary, but by the intensified research and merchandising efforts of individual companies hard at work providing new products for a steadily growing number of consumers.

4. Pension funds will continue to provide a large flow of savings for investment in all kinds of securities—although the rate of increase in such investments will be far less dramatic than during the postwar period to date. A large portion of these funds will continue to be invested in common stocks, except in unusual periods, like 1970, when interest rates go through the roof. The flow of funds into equities from this and other institutional sources will be sufficient to maintain price-earnings ratios at current, rather low levels, and if and when individual buyers return to the market, price-earnings ratios will go up.

5. Once again, in recent troubled years, the political and economic system demonstrated its resiliency. Despite an unusual and foreboding conjuncture of political, social, and financial difficulties, *the system survived*. The Vietnam war is ending. Racial inequities are gradually being corrected. Greater awareness of environmental problems will lead to the solution of those problems. The campuses are calm. On Wall Street a financial disaster has been averted. The financial community is reforming and restructuring to respond to its public responsibilities. Investor confidence is returning. (We should make clear we do not necessarily espouse this

optimistic line of thought, *but investors may,* and that is what makes markets go up.)

Among the contrary arguments are:

1. Newly perceived social needs—for more effective education, better health care, more and better urban housing, improved transportation, the protection of the environment—will create such persistent demand for funds from all levels of government that long-range interest rates will stay high. Fixed-income securities will remain relatively attractive as an alternative to common stocks, and price-earnings ratios will drift *down,* not up, until stock values once again establish themselves as "reasonable" in relation to other opportunities (perhaps when dividend returns climb to 5 to 6 percent).

2. The needs described above may call for higher taxes; while these might take some pressure off interest rates, they could interrupt corporate earnings growth.

3. The inability of governments throughout the developed industrial world to devise effective policies to control "cost-push" inflation, either in the unionized manufacturing sector or in the nonunionized service sector of the economies in question, will create (if it has not done so already) widespread concern that inflation is here to stay. This will, in turn, produce a speculative bias in our economy and our financial markets as corporations and individuals struggle to protect themselves against such inflation. Such hedging may, in the first instance, involve flight from fixed-income securities—a widespread desire to borrow money rather than to invest in securities with a fixed return, which in an inflationary world provide a dwindling real return. It may also involve renewed speculative interest in equities. This scenario calls for a gradual deterioration in present wage-price controls, a return of an inflationary psychology, another dramatic rise in interest rates, and a repetition of the 1970 financial fiasco as investors run, finally, from speculatively inflated common stocks toward greater liquidity and safety. The continuing high level of personal savings may reflect lingering fear about inflation and unemployment.

4. Growing concern about the quality of the environment will

exert new, complex pressures to prevent continued (almost automatic) growth in real Gross National Product of the sort we have come to assume in the postwar period in the United States, indeed in the entire Western world. Population growth is slowing, and it may indeed occasionally stop. Increased attention will be paid to the composition rather than the size of GNP. Uncertainty about these matters will cause investors to pay less for long-term growth potential than in the past, and the consequence, again, will be lower price-earnings ratios.

5. The competitiveness of the United States economy and the dollar has been eroding. Our large trade surpluses have disappeared. Protectionist pressures are mounting, as in the 1930s. Large balance-of-payment deficits may continue, even with realigned exchange rates. The long-range implications of these trends, if permitted to continue indefinitely, are difficult to gauge, both for economies throughout the free world and for individual companies. But at the very least they represent a large area of economic uncertainty.

6. Major U.S. corporations, which were in superb financial condition not many years ago, are no longer in such condition (although admittedly they are in better shape than in 1970). Many have relied unduly on short- and long-range borrowing in recent years. Despite recent refinancings, many companies will have to rely on common stock financing more heavily in the years ahead than in the 1960s. This will increase the supply of equities and may put pressure on price-earnings ratios.

The case *against* investment in common stocks seems to the authors more compelling than it would have seemed, say, in 1965, when one could have marshaled half a dozen or so positive arguments and only two negative ones (climbing interest rates and balance-of-payments difficulties). On the other hand, the fact that negative factors are more widely appreciated, better understood, and more readily articulated than in 1965 suggests that perhaps these risks have already been partly reflected in—*discounted by*—market prices.

Is the case against common stocks sufficiently compelling to stop this book right here? We think not.

In the first place, it is not a question of investors putting *all* their money in common stocks. We favor investing gradually, over a relatively long period of time, to minimize the risks of misreading the underlying economic situation at a given moment.

Second, we have never believed it made much sense for the investor to "play the market" as a whole. Instead, we stress selection of soundly financed, carefully managed companies in relatively promising businesses. This approach has served investors in good stead indeed historically, even during the last seven years, despite unforeseen turmoil in virtually all domestic financial markets. We believe such selectivity—a word that tends on Wall Street to become a cliché rather than a discipline—still holds the key to future success.

In a trillion-dollar economy there are bound to be continuing emerging trends that create favorable investment opportunities. Witness the emergence of such newer fields of investment attention as mobile homes, institutional food servicing, environmental controls, hospital management, and real estate development as areas in which selective investors have made good returns.

In our judgment, investors should seek, and still can obtain, an annual return of 10 to 12 percent from dividends and capital gains combined (on a pre-income-tax basis) from a carefully selected list of common stocks during the years immediately ahead. This is a reasonable expectation, in our view, in relationship to:

1. *Returns now available from other, less risky investments.* The 10 to 12 percent return we prescribe is at least double that provided by savings accounts, Treasury bills, and other relatively liquid, safe fixed-income investments; and about 50 percent more than the return provided by longer-term, high-quality bonds (which, as we have witnessed in the postwar period, are not riskless either).

2. *Desired protection from inflation.* Assuming that inflation continues at a rate averaging 3 to 4 percent, a 10 to 12 percent

return from common stocks provides a *real* return of about 7 percent per annum. A savings account providing a total return of 4 to 5 percent provides a *real* return, after allowing for inflation, of only 1 to 2 percent. *Adjusted for the inflation factor, then, the 10 to 12 percent return from equities looks a good deal better relative to alternatives than it does on a gross basis.*

3. *The realities of economic growth in the United States.* We believe that *real* growth in Gross National Product is likely to amount to more than 3 percent per annum over the next decade, despite the uncertainties (environmental concern, slower population growth, increased foreign competition, etc.) already cited. The 6 to 8 percent *real* return we regard as reasonable from equities reflects the effective application of choice. We intend to help investors improve their analytical skills so they will pick only the most promising, most soundly managed businesses in the most interesting, trouble-free industries—in short, those whose earnings can grow faster than the economy for a long time.

Why not shoot for more? Isn't 10 to 12 percent per annum pretty tame? Well, we may be tame, but we see no evidence that investors—individual or institutional—can consistently earn, say, a 15 to 20 percent annual rate of return from common stocks. Many professional (institutional) investors came to the conclusion in recent years that they could and should generate such high returns on money for their clients. There were several reasons for this belief, and they are instructive:

1. A number of corporations appeared successful in generating earnings growth of this order of magnitude or higher, some through a process of genuinely innovative internal growth, others as a result of living in a booming inflationary economy, and still others through acquisitions combined with accounting legerdemain.

2. Institutional demand for common shares pushed stock prices up, so that in many cases stock prices went up faster than earnings.

3. Professional investors, toward the end of the period, were *forced* to pursue these higher returns (15 percent plus) from common stocks because returns from fixed-income securities had

risen strikingly. There was no apparent reason to invest in common stocks if one could make only, say, 10 percent per annum.

In fact, in an economy growing at more than 3 percent in real terms and with inflation of 3 to 4 percent superimposed on top of it, it is unrealistic to expect any major segment of the economy to provide growth at twice that rate, i.e., 15 percent per annum, for long. Investors should ask themselves how they can reasonably expect to earn 15 percent returns from investments in corporations which themselves are not making that kind of return on investment in their own businesses. Of *Fortune*'s 500 largest companies, only 57 in 1970 were able to earn a return of 15 percent on their stockholders' equity. Still fewer earned 15 percent on total invested capital.

Over the long run, there must be a correlation between economic growth, the rates of return earned by corporations, and the rates of return earned by investors.

If interest rates should again begin climbing, and if you find you again have the opportunity to make a 9 or 10 or 11 percent return from high-quality long-term corporate bonds, or a 7 or 8 percent return from shorter-term fixed-income investments, and thus are confronted with the choice of reaching for unrealistic returns from common equities or simply abandoning the exercise of selecting and owning stocks, then *abandon the exercise*. Sell your common stocks. Raise cash. Invest it in short-term savings accounts or long-term bonds—provided they are liquid enough for you to sell when the situation changes.

Similarly, if interest rates decline further, you may be in a position to settle for 8 to 10 percent returns from common stocks and still do enough better, relatively, to make the investments worthwhile.

To conclude: the 10 to 12 percent return we cite as reasonable today may not be reasonable tomorrow. The concept of earning a reasonable return is not static. In determining what is a "fair" return, investors must look not only at the prospects for their own carefully chosen individual investments but at investments available in other markets as well.

PHILOSOPHY

3

What Kinds of Companies Should You Own?

Having established reasonable objectives, how does one begin selecting specific stocks? At the risk of oversimplification, we believe you have two alternatives.

You can buy stocks of successful companies. These are companies that have already demonstrated their ability to grow consistently and rapidly and earn high returns on their invested capital despite turmoil in the economy and the marketplace. They appear to have a remarkable degree of control over their own destinies. What provides that control we shall come to in due course.

Or you can buy the stocks of problem companies—companies in which this control does not show and probably does not exist. Included in this category are companies ranging from the almost successful to the desperately ill.

We realize that this division of the stock market into two clearly defined camps, the "good guys" and the "bad guys," is simplistic. An infinite variety of degrees of success, and of failure, comprise the universe of corporate enterprise. Nevertheless, we believe this is a *useful* distinction. In investments, as in other endeavors, one learns more from a study of the spectacular triumphs and failures than from an analysis of mediocrity.

Let us start with the successful company. We strongly believe that the *major* portion of your portfolio should comprise a diversified selection of successful companies.

What do we mean by a "successful" company? When we talk about successful companies, we are referring to those that meet certain criteria *today,* not five years ago or even last year. Our job, furthermore, is not only to determine whether a company is trouble free or problematical today, but also to gauge the direction in which it is now moving. General Motors is unquestionably one of the most successful companies that has ever evolved in the history of this country, but where is it going, and taking investors, today? Few, if any, industries or companies stand absolutely still; the fundamentals improve or they worsen. The changes occurring in the thousands of companies that make up the stock market are like those taking place in a wine cellar. Some of the wines are growing old but not great. Some will achieve greatness slowly and retain it for a number of years. Others will gain and lose it quickly. A few, like the sherries and Madeiras, are great now and will stay that way for generations. Some wines in the cellar were once great but now are over the hill (beware of these, the overpriced blue chips).

The difference, of course, is that the wines change in a controlled environment; the companies that make up the stock market live in a more capricious world.

There are a number of dramatic examples of successful companies. They appear to have a common characteristic: the *consistency* with which they have been able to increase their earnings year after year. Despite fluctuations in the business cycle, despite the rise and fall of specific products, despite the changing wage-price structure, despite foreign competition, they move steadily ahead, outperforming the average corporation.

IBM has depended principally on a continuously expanding base of lease rentals and a worldwide marketing organization in the data-processing industry. Avon has found a unique merchandising technique for promoting cosmetic products. Johnson & Johnson has taken a domestic health-care market and widened its horizon throughout the free world. Procter & Gamble, with eighteen straight years of rising sales, earnings, and dividends, has steadily added new products which have soon dominated their markets (the detergent Tide, Pampers disposable diapers, Bounty paper towels) here and abroad. Tampax has concentrated on a unique approach to feminine hygiene, and has built a powerful, proprietary brand-name image throughout the world. Lubrizol has built upon a specific market for chemical additives for the automobile industry, a growing worldwide market dependent on new chemical combinations (more than half its sales come from products developed in the past five years). Through acquisitions, ITT has assembled a large and prosperous family of companies in service and manufacturing businesses.

As previously noted, there are many kinds of problem companies, ranging from the temporary to the endemic.

Least problematical are those companies that stumble because of temporary internal dislocations. From these one-shot problems frequently emerge dramatic investment opportunities. These companies enjoy good management. They innovate. They have adequate financial resources. Sometimes their disruptions are caused by human failures that are correctable: unanticipated dislocations attributable to undigested acquisitions or to excessive additions to plant capacity. Recent experiences of Rubbermaid Corporation and the Amerada Hess Corporation illustrate the point.

In 1968 Rubbermaid brought several large new plants on-stream together. A combination of start-up expenses at these new plants and changes in second- and third-echelon management caused a decline in profit margins and earnings (sales did well). Management openly acknowledged the existence of these problems. "We simply tried to do too much too fast," admitted President Don Noble. The stock market acknowledged the lower earnings with lower stock prices. The company moved to resolve its internal difficulties, and as new plant capacity was utilized, profit margins not only recovered but reached new high levels, producing record corporate profits. As the company's strengths reasserted themselves, investors were presented with a dramatic investment opportunity. Management's frank treatment of its problems, accompanied by a demonstrated turnaround in margins and earnings, restored the market's confidence, and the stock has since done exceedingly well.

Amerada Hess represents another case of imprudent market judgment. All through the period of Hess's courtship of Amerada, the former company's earnings grew rapidly, with attendant stock price advances. Then, after a hectic final pursuit, with accompanying counterproposals and a dramatic tender offer by another corporation, the marriage of the two companies was consummated in 1969. In the months after the merger the new management was faced with a number of problems, including a costly delay in the opening of a new refinery and a series of write-offs resulting from the merger. The Libyan political revolution further impaired the market's confidence in the future earnings growth of the combined companies. The consequence was a drastic decline in the price of the shares of Amerada Hess common from a high of 61 for Hess shortly before the merger to a low of 20 approximately one year later.

When the dust had settled, the market's doubts proved to be unjustified. The new refinery came on-stream shortly; the expected benefits of the merger began to be realized; the Libyan uncertainties, while still very much there, did not prevent a dramatic improvement in earnings in 1970, only one year later than earlier predicted; and the shares of the company recovered handsomely. The stock market's unwillingness to overlook temporary internal problems and to anticipate eventual recovery—its superficial evaluation of the underlying facts—caused a dislocation which some investors converted into an investment opportunity.

Both Rubbermaid and Amerada Hess were successful companies in temporary disguise.

Then there are the companies whose problems are chiefly external, usually of an industry nature. Many of our larger companies suffer from these difficulties. Chronic overcapacity, combined with growing low-cost foreign competition, has plagued the chemical, aluminum, paper, and steel industries. Du Pont, Alcoa, International Paper, and U.S. Steel are all perennial victims of industry-wide distress.

Recent classic examples of companies with internal problems of greater persistence than the ones we discussed earlier (the cases of Rubbermaid and Amerada Hess) are Penn Central and Lockheed. In the first instance poor management led to bankruptcy; in the second the company hovers on the edge and the final story remains untold.

Unlike the merger of Hess Oil and Amerada, the marriage of the Pennsylvania Railroad to the New York Central did not produce the growth or the economies of scale which are necessary for a successful consolidation. Mesmerized by huge nonrailroad assets and the glamour of diversification, inept management misapplied resources and neglected the primary business.

In the case of Lockheed, management consistently underestimated the costs of new military and commercial aircraft. Under the assumption that its significant contribution to national defense would see it through its difficulties, it bought business that was not economic and dissipated its assets. Everybody was fooled. Despite governmental assistance, the company is not out of the woods. Even if it survives, is it likely to be a rewarding investment?

Are these problem companies good investments? Can they be turned around? Such equities are gambles, not sound investments. One should commit only a small portion of his resources to this type of problem company and then only after structuring a powerful portfolio of successful companies. While the rewards may be handsome if the turnaround is achieved, the odds are always long.

Admittedly, there are examples of successful recovery from several problems—some improvements temporary, some apparently sustainable. In its postwar history Chrysler has had several rebirths, only to fall back into disarray. In the early sixties Chrysler's directors made constructive management changes. The Rockefeller interests moved into the picture; George Love, able leader of Consolidated Coal, an associate of the late George Humphrey, entered the picture and was made chairman of the board; and Lynn Townsend, then administrative vice president, became president. Styling improved. Costs were reduced, dealerships strengthened. And the external factors affecting the company took a turn for the better, too. Factory sales of United States passenger cars moved up steadily from 5.5 million in 1961 to nearly 8 million in 1964. Chrysler improved its market penetration. Earnings rose from $0.30 per share in 1961 to a peak of $5.50 per share in 1964, and the stock catapulted from a low of 9⅞ to a high of 65¼. Then troubles reappeared. Costs skyrocketed. Lower-priced foreign cars from Europe and Japan increased their share of the United States market and forced changes in styling and market share of the U.S. manufacturers. Chrysler was unable to sustain its improved position. Earnings disappeared once again, the company's financial position deteriorated, and the prospects for fundamental improvement are cloudy. The stock has fallen from 72 (in 1968) to as low as 16 (in 1970).

S. S. Kresge, on the other hand, emerged from an arteriosclerotic condition which characterized the variety-store business in the 1950s and early 1960s to become an outstanding example of a company whose management identified changing conditions, adapted its business to a new environment, and entirely from within created new corporate momentum. Kresge reduced its traditional variety-store business by closing over two hundred of its least profitable units, established its K-Mart discount stores as the most successful national chain of discount stores, identified the fastest-growing areas of the country, concentrated its efforts in these areas, and centralized its purchasing and administrative controls more effectively than any other retailer. Its sales rose from $426 million in 1961 to $2.6 billion in 1970; its earnings have increased from $0.27 per share to $1.85 per share in these years without interruption, and the stock has risen from 4⅝ to a price of 98 in 1971.

In 1969, as the U.S. economy slowed, Kresge experienced a

sudden and unexpected profit-margin squeeze. The company reported an earnings gain smaller than investors expected. The market reacted violently downward to disappointing news. During 1970 the company coped with economic recession by adopting stringent cost controls and generated a strong earnings improvement in an indifferent retail environment. This reestablished the market's confidence in management. Kresge is a successful company by our definition of the term.

Looking back on the companies we have just discussed, one is struck by the number of successful companies that have built strong positions outside the United States. They tend to dominate world markets as well as local markets. Many of the problem companies, on the other hand, are those most adversely affected by imports.

Management's ability to respond to change, and to make earnings grow consistently even in a difficult environment, is the critical feature of a successful company.

Common stocks must be looked at in a particular way: not as "assets in the ground," not as "inflation hedges," or "income producers," but as the end results of the combined efforts of groups of talented human beings. We invest in managerial skills: in scientific and engineering talent, merchandising experience, financial competence. Successful companies have these combined abilities in demonstrated abundance, and they apply them in fields of great promise.

The human talent on which you have placed your bet constantly creates new values—new products, new services, and new markets—that make the company grow. Sometimes the speed with which it does so is breathtaking, as was the case with Xerox; sometimes it is more modest but is regular and consistent in its pace, as with Lubrizol, Johnson & Johnson, or 3M.

You are faced, of course, with a cruel dilemma in your choice between these two kinds of investments: When you identify a successful company, you will almost certainly find that its success has already been at least partly signaled by the market. Its stock has probably already moved up. So-called professional investors will be lamenting the high price-earnings ratio at which it sells. In short, the successful company will almost always look too "dear." In contrast, the problem company's shares may be selling at a price that takes into account ("discounts," in Wall Street parlance) all problems and no solutions. For this reason, it is statistically enticing.

We beg you not to be frightened away from the successful companies *simply* because they sell at high price-earnings ratios. These companies have talented managements; they are innovators; they operate in large markets; they have a remarkable degree of control over their destinies compared to the typical business concern. If this is true, why should they sell at low price-earnings ratios?

Don't automatically succumb, as so many investors do, to "market acrophobia," a paralysis resulting from the fact that a stock may already have made someone else a lot of money.

Approach these issues with an open mind. Ask yourself: How long will the company in question have to be successful in order for the stock to keep going up? What are its chances of doing so? Successful companies sell at a high price-earnings ratio for a reason: investors are optimistic about the outlook. Sometimes the optimism is justified, sometimes not.

Be patient! If a successful company—that is, one whose earnings keep rising, whose products are in demand, whose costs are under control—doesn't appreciate at once, exercise self-discipline. Successful investing takes time.

Not all companies that sell at high price-earnings ratios are successful; in later chapters, you will see that a number of them are problem companies in disguise. The successful company selling at a low price-earnings ratio is a rarer species.

Above all, be flexible. You build a degree of flexibility into your investment strategy by not plunging into the market too quickly and by keeping some of your money elsewhere. Most important is a continuously flexible, inquiring attitude toward individual stocks. Occasionally, *even with an open mind,* you will be forced to admit that the stock of a particular successful company is too high; this comes not from a fear of heights but from common sense. Sometimes successful companies as a group are overpriced, as in late 1969 and 1970. (Witness the correction in price of almost all growth stocks which occurred during that period. And what opportunities were presented by this adjustment!) If, during such a hiatus, you can find a reasonably priced problem company that appears to be coming to life, you can probably more productively employ your capital, for the time being, in that arena.* By so doing you provide yourself with the psychological diversification discussed in a later chapter.

We see the role of the problem company in your portfolio, then, as that of an interim holding—an investment stopgap upon which you rely, opportunistically, when the companies that you intend to make the backbone of your portfolio are selling at prices that are truly too dear.

Some years ago, a large, well-known, and well-managed investment trust reported to shareholders on several occasions as follows:

Natural resource stocks are believed the best insurance in a world in which no nation has yet solved the problem of vigorous growth without inflation. Growth stocks are held when available at multiples of earnings that do not assume unchecked growth into the distant future.

This is a flexible approach. There is clearly room for a number of different types of stocks in the fund; its managers' minds are not closed either to successful companies or to problem companies (to reduce it to our simple terminology). Yet we believe the emphasis is wrong. Common stocks should not be viewed primarily as insurance—whether it be insurance against inflation or against some other evil. The experience of 1969 and 1970 exposed the fallibility of the theory that common stocks of any kind are adequate protection against inflation. On a short-term basis the op-

---

* You may also conclude that under these conditions the whole market is too high and that the solution is to have less money in it.

posite proved true. As inflation accelerated, the efforts taken to "cool it" increased interest rates and reduced business demand. Both conditions hurt corporate earnings and stock prices. (Whether corporate earnings will flourish in the world of wage-price constraints—the latest official response to inflation—remains to be seen.) You will do better over the long run, as you struggle with the problem of investment selection, if you view common stocks as *capital-building opportunities,* whether or not we have inflation. In the terminology of the fund in question, this philosophy can be summarized as follows:

In a world increasingly characterized by man's ability to engineer change, the best profit opportunities exist in the stocks of companies managed by people who are able, to an unusual degree, to create and then dominate large new markets. When such stocks are not available on rational statistical terms, the stocks of other companies with less adequate resources, whether human or natural, should be held on an interim basis, providing they are available at prices that reflect their more limited long-term potentials. If common stocks appear unreasonably priced, and you are willing to accept the capital-gains tax consequence, you can reduce your equity investments, and find alternatives in short- or long-term fixed-income securities.

SELECTION

4

The Ingredients of Corporate Success: The Power of Innovation

In the previous chapter we described successful companies as having "a remarkable degree of control over their own destinies." We then paraded a group of terms such as "talented management," "rapidly growing earnings," "large markets," etc., some of which are causes and others results of the "remarkable degree of control." Now we want to elaborate.

To begin with, all successful companies innovate.

In its simplest form, innovation requires the introduction of new products and services, which are better—that is, cheaper, faster, easier to use, more flexible, etc.—than the competitors'. Often they are unique, sometimes creating markets that did not previously exist.

In an analysis of creativity, Jerome S. Bruner, professor of psychology at Harvard, says that the hallmark of a creative enterprise is "the effective surprise."

The Xerox 914 Copier was an "effective surprise." Introduced in the spring of 1960, the 914 was the only office copier that made copies on ordinary paper, that could make more than one copy without the operator rehandling the original document, and that could copy from three-dimensional objects (which meant that the user could make a copy of a magazine article, for example, without clipping the article out of the magazine).

The 914 gave Xerox a critical competitive edge in the office-copying market in the early sixties and enabled it to build a powerful marketing force. During the 1960s the company introduced and effectively marketed succeeding generations of xerographic copying devices—some faster, some smaller—and growingly sophisticated peripheral devices. These improvements enormously enlarged the market, so that the company served not only the office-copying market but the short-run printing market as well. In 1960 Xerox (then Haloid Xerox) had revenues of $30 million. In 1970 its xerographic copying products alone generated estimated revenues of $1.4 billion and earnings in excess of $100 million.

The Polaroid Land camera is another major "effective surprise." Since the introduction of the camera in the late forties, the company (not unlike Xerox) has developed and marketed a variety of evolutionary products, all relying on Dr. Edwin L. Land's original concept of instant photography but often involving major breakthroughs in different fields of research. The development of instant color photographs, the continued upgrading of all aspects of the camera mechanisms (shutters, lenses, etc.), and the gradual penetration of overseas markets have enabled Polaroid's worldwide sales to surpass the half-billion-dollar mark and earnings to approach $60 million.

Now we await the introduction of still more new products from the company, in the form of instant color transparencies, instant color motion pictures, and a wallet-size pocket camera (called "the Aladdin") for instant color or black-and-white photos, utilizing a new color negative compound which some expect will make obsolete all Land films now on the market. Will these new "effective surprises" propel Polaroid through another stage of worldwide expansion? No one knows, but expectations are high.

In the wings there stands, for the first time, a threat to Polaroid's monopoly in the instant-photography field. Kodak, acknowledging that this "effective surprise" now shares the camera market with it, has promised to introduce an instant-photographic product in the next few years.

One could list other effective corporate innovations that have conquered the marketplace in recent decades: among them, Sony's tape recorders, G. D. Searle's contraceptive pills, Bausch & Lomb's new "Soflens" contact eyeglasses, and Procter & Gamble's disposable diapers. However, the "effective surprise" doesn't necessarily take the form of products, e.g., tangible goods. It often manifests itself as a new marketing technique, or a new method of *combining products with distribution* that no one else has used in quite the same way or on such an ambitious scale before.

Avon Products, IBM, and, more recently, McDonald's are outstanding, although different, examples of companies that allied products and distribution in new and potent form.

There is nothing technically unique about Avon cosmetics; and there are many other door-to-door selling organizations. The fortuitous blend of the two is what is effective. Women like to try new cosmetics in private, to experiment where they have room and time. In her home, with no competing products to distract her, in the soothing and reassuring hands of her Avon representative, who provides undivided attention, the typical housewife can be persuaded to buy often enough to provide Avon a handsome return.

In recent years Avon's door-to-door selling force has become so large and effective that it is sometimes said that "Avon is a door-to-door company that just happens to be in the cosmetics business," the implication being that it could use its powerful marketing force to sell anything from pretzels to vacuum cleaners. In recent years the company has supplemented its cosmetics lines with miscellaneous household products—air sprays, insect repellents, etc. It has also begun to sell costume jewelry and has test-marketed the sale of greeting cards. Nevertheless, the "effective surprise" that gave the company its first "leg up" was the unique combination of cosmetics and door-to-door selling.

IBM did not move far, far ahead of its competitors in the computer industry in the 1950s because of a unique—or even a superior—piece of hardware. In the early days Sperry Rand held this role, and in later years a number of companies—Burroughs, Control Data, Honeywell—introduced individual pieces of computer hardware that outperformed their IBM counterparts. However, IBM understood what the customer wanted—a solution to his data-processing problems—and it understood that the solution required not only a computer but a computer the customer would understand how to use. Thus since 1950 the company has been engaged in one of the most extraordinary customer hand-holding operations in history. The IBM computer has been backed by computer programs, compilers, systems engineers, and of course servicemen to keep the hardware working—again a marriage of product with distribution to provide a convincing competitive superiority.

Increasingly, "effective surprise" appears to be manifesting itself in the consumer goods and consumer service areas of the economy. Again, the successful companies aren't necessarily providing anything new (nothing new, for example, about food or lodgings or night watchmen), but they are making the services available in new ways and on a scale not contemplated by their predecessors.

Isn't there a difference, for example, between the old-fashioned Mom & Pop hamburger stand and McDonald's? Or between the old-fashioned downtown hotels and a typical Holiday Inn motel?

The newer organizations are applying to the service field the techniques utilized by manufacturing companies since the industrial revolution. These techniques involve: (1) *standardization of products and facilities* (over 8 billion McDonald's hamburgers, all alike, and 1,346* Holiday Inn motels, if not identical, all recognizably similar); and (2) *specialization of labor.* The latter comes into play not only in the production of the standardized products and facilities but in the way employees are trained, services are priced, and customers treated. The developments are not unlike those that earlier provided explosive growth for merchandising and food chains like Sears and Safeway, but they tend today to involve more specialization of services or products offered; and they are often related to recent cultural changes—the spectacular growth, for example, in automobile travel and leisure time.

* As of October 1, 1971.

The same rationalizing process is at work in the provision of services in various commercial (as distinct from consumer) markets. ARA Services, for example, dominates the field of institutional food service. It provides such service to corporations, schools, colleges, hospitals, and governmental agencies. Sales of this company have increased from $63.7 million to $648.4 million in the last ten years, and earnings growth has been equally impressive.

The same kinds of customers need protection from all forms of criminal trespass, and the hundred-year-old Pinkerton's has answered the call for protective services. The corporate and institutional customer also has mundane but necessary requirements in the field of maintenance. A growing industry has emerged of which concerns like Allied Maintenance and Prudential Building Maintenance are among the most successful. The provision of *management* services to private hospitals is still another growing market of this nature.

In each of these cases the specialized seller of services is able to concentrate his energies on all the details of his business— recruitment, training, purchase of materials, control of costs—in a manner that the individual customer cannot possibly emulate. Often these service companies take headaches away from their customers, free up time, and by operating on a large scale, offer dependability and attractive price, thus creating new growth opportunities.

Peter Drucker, an imaginative management consultant, describes another, still more subtle, form of innovation in his book *Managing for Results.** This is "the ability to envisage as a system what to others are unrelated, separate elements."

General Motors did just that in 1921.

At the time, the company was floundering. Ford had 60 percent of the passenger car and truck market, and Chevrolet 4 percent. GM had just undergone a turbulent management change, with William Durant moving out of and Alfred Sloan up into the

* New York: Harper & Row, 1964.

higher command. Under Sloan, the company appointed a special committee of "experienced automobile men" to look into "product policy." As Sloan says in his book, *My Years with General Motors,** "This task was to be one of the most significant in the evolution of the corporation."

Let us keep quoting him:

> The product policy we proposed is the one for which General Motors has now long been known. We said first that the corporation should produce a line of cars in each price area . . . , second, that the price steps should not be such as to leave wide gaps in the line, and yet should be great enough to keep their numbers within reason . . . , and third, that there should be no duplication by the corporation in the price fields or steps. . . .
>
> In the perspective of so many years gone by, the idea of this policy seems pretty simple, like a shoe manufacturer proposing to sell shoes in more than one size. But it did not seem simple at the time, when Ford had more than half the market with two grades (the high-volume, low-priced Model T and the low-volume high-priced Lincoln). . . .
>
> We proposed in general that General Motors should place its cars at the top of each price range and make them of such a quality that they would attract sales from below that price, selling to those customers who might be willing to pay a little more for the additional quality, and attract sales also from above that price, selling to those customers who would see the price advantage in a car of close to the quality of higher-priced competition.

As Mr. Sloan says, none of this seems dramatic today. All the major domestic automobile producers follow the same marketing strategy, with varying degrees of success, and consumers and investors take it for granted. But in 1921 the Model T and the Lincoln were "unrelated, separate elements," and it took General Motors to merge these and other "elements" into a "system." The originality of this strategy perhaps can be measured best by its impact on Ford, which did not or would not see the handwriting on the wall and sank into a prolonged torpor from which it did not recover until after World War II.

* New York: Doubleday & Co., 1964.

IBM has followed the General Motors approach for some time, most recently, in 1970, with the introduction of the 370 series and the System 3 computers. It has built a powerful "system" of data-processing services and devices, integrated from the smallest to the largest machines and permitting—in fact, encouraging—the customer to "upgrade" to faster, more flexible hardware as requirements change and grow.

In the retailing and consumer service field, Sears has succeeded in harnessing a number of widely disparate elements into a coherent whole. Starting primarily as a mail-order house catering to the rural population, the company has evolved into a seller to practically everybody: farmers, factory workers, suburban housewives, and urban sophisticates. Its products range from denim overalls to fur coats, from dishwashers to abstract paintings. Its services include automobile lubrication centers, travel bureaus, and insurance offices.

Probably no company has been more adept at keeping up with the rapid pace of change in the past decade than International Telephone & Telegraph. ITT appears to have succeeded brilliantly in incorporating under one roof most of the elements of business which have emerged as interesting new growth markets in recent years. Starting with a profitable international sales base in telecommunications and an unsatisfactory domestic business, Harold Geneen, ITT's hard-working chief executive officer, has built, without question, the world's largest service organization: finance, insurance, and mutual fund management (Thorp Finance, Hartford Fire Insurance, and Hamilton Management Corporation), hotels (Sheraton Corporation of America), land improvement and residential community developments (Levitt & Sons), automobile rentals and airport parking services (Avis, Inc., and Apcoa), fire protection services (Grinnell Corporation), and food processing and services (Continental Baking and Canteen Corporation).* No

* Under a consent decree issued in 1971, ITT has agreed to divest itself within two years of Canteen Corporation, the fire protection division of Grinnell, and within three years to divest either Avis Rent A Car, Levitt &

other corporation has been able to blend so many disparate entities into such an apparently integrated business with sustained growth. We use the word "apparently" because it remains to be seen whether these various organizations are truly integrated or depend crucially on the energy and genius of Mr. Geneen.

We started by saying that successful companies innovate. We conclude by observing three kinds of innovators: (1) those that introduce specific products and services, ranging from superior to unique; (2) those that go a step further and combine new products and services into a package that is not elsewhere for sale, or not in the same way or on the same scale; and (3) those that go still further and combine a seemingly infinite—and to the struggling competitor, seemingly impossible—number of products, services, and packages into what comes close to being an all-powerful system. The duration of a company's success depends importantly on its ability to progress from the more simple to the more sophisticated forms of innovation during its business life.

Sons, Hamilton Life, and Life Insurance Company of New York; or Hartford Fire Insurance.

ITT will exercise the first series of options and retain Hartford Fire. This will reduce volume at current rates of revenue about $1 billion annually.

5

The Ingredients of Corporate Success: Staying Power in the Marketplace

O f course, it helps if a company innovates in a market of some size. And it helps still more if the nature of its innovative effort is such that it gives the company a stranglehold on the market.

As we see it, then, the second and third distinguishing characteristics of the enduringly successful company are: *it serves a large and growing market,* and *once entrenched, it is difficult to dislodge.*

There are two fundamental difficulties associated with our investment philosophy, that of investing in successful, or growth, companies as opposed to investing in neglected, troublesome, "undervalued" companies (the philosophy espoused by many Wall Street old-timers). One of these difficulties* involves measuring the size of the market in which a truly innovative company operates. If the company is truly innovative, the product is brand-new, and the needs it serves may be new (or at least previously unperceived). How, then, can one tell how much of the product will be bought, how large the market will be, and how long it will keep growing?

Sperry Rand once predicted that the total demand for large computers would amount to four! Shortly after the advent of the 914 Copier, however, Xerox perceived that its market was huge.

* The second is discussed in Chapter 9.

With sales of about $30 million annually in the early sixties, it confidently and accurately forecast annual revenues of $1 billion in less than ten years! The investors who bet against Sperry Rand, and for the more imaginative IBM, did well. Those who took the risk that Xerox management was right—not just smoking pot (if managements smoked pot, in those days)—did brilliantly.

But it's a tricky matter.

Gauging the size of the market for a new product is one of the most difficult tasks confronting the investor. What is the ultimate potential for xerographic copying devices or for instant photography? Will "Soflens" eventually replace all existing contact lenses, and conventional eyeglasses as well? Will we have video cassettes in every home? How can you tell?

You can't, really. Certainly not with any precision. After all, the managements of the companies that bring out these products frequently don't know themselves.

Broadly based companies like Avon, IBM, and General Motors operate in well-defined industry groups: cosmetics, office equipment, and automobiles. You know that these industries are large (each generates billions of dollars in annual revenues) and that they grow. In the financial sections of the daily newspaper, in weekly magazines, and in more specialized trade papers there appears a steady stream of data pertaining to the projected growth rates of these and other major industries. The research department of your brokerage firm undoubtedly has additional information of this sort. Monthly bank letters and special economic services provide similar projections. You will find that, with relatively few exceptions, there is a rough consensus. At the moment, for example, most experts believe dollar revenues of the office equipment industry are growing at a 10 to 15 percent annual rate; cosmetics, 8 to 10 percent. Services as a whole are growing at a 7 to 8 percent rate, faster than the economy as a whole, with many individual services moving ahead at a still more rapid pace.

A great deal of professional work on the part of many first-rate economists goes into these forecasts, and we don't see much point in the lay investor challenging them unless he has a strong conviction that certain underlying assumptions are wrong. In order to hold such a conviction, he must have a particularly favorable vantage point from which to view an industry's prospects. (He is a metal broker or a buyer for a retail store, for example, and he sees with his own eyes that demand and price patterns are different from what the economists say. Or his broker is backed up by a research specialist intimately enough acquainted with his industry to challenge the forecaster.) If you are in this position, by all means take advantage of it. Otherwise, leave the broad industrial forecasting to the experts.

Admittedly, the experts are having more difficulty coming to grips with overall forecasts—for the economy as a whole and for major sectors of it—than ten or twenty years ago. Computerized economic models produce more forecasts than formerly, but these are far from foolproof; they must be revised—like all forecasts— as changes take place in demographic trends, fiscal and monetary policy, or consumer expectations. Major questions exist about the future rate of growth in productivity (is the "Puritan ethic" breaking down, and if so, what are the implications for corporate efficiency?); and the impact of a variety of political, social, and cultural forces on production and consumption patterns.

Nevertheless, you will still have to rely on the experts, and on a good deal of common sense, for forecasts of overall economic growth and for insights into which industries, which sectors, are likely to grow faster or slower than the economy as a whole.

Your troubles are more complex with the smaller companies that occupy a segment—sometimes a very narrow one—of the large industries, or that are in newer industries which they themselves have created. What really is the market for chemical additives for lubricants and fuels, and where does Lubrizol fit into the market? If, in 1970, 45 percent of this company's products contained chemical ingredients created during the last five years, who is to say what can be created during the next five years? Several years ago the world's leading petroleum economists began to project a gradual decline in the annual rate of increase in petroleum consumption at home and abroad. Since then the growth in consumption has confounded the experts by its strength, and the disparity between forecast and reality has created the possibility of a world energy shortage. On the other hand, uncertainties raised by drug researchers about the medical side effects of birth control pills have slowed the acceptance of this product in recent years, disappointing the prognostications of the experts. Similarly, the recent leveling-off in demand for Polaroid cameras has raised questions about the fundamental nature of the instant-photography market—its price elasticity and its relevance to consumer styles and tastes in the seventies.

In order to come to grips with this problem, let us look at the various types of market growth that can propel a company forward, rather than try to determine the exact dollar potential for a specific product some years down the road. If we can satisfy ourselves, on a common-sense basis, that the *nature* of a particular company's growth is such that it should continue indefinitely, or until certain specific, *recognizable* changes take place, we may have all the information we need to make a judgment about growth prospects.

First, there are markets that grow more or less parallel with the population. (There are some, of course, that grow more slowly, but let's assume they're in the buggy whip category—unsexy, at least for investment purposes.) The beer industry is a case in point. Per capita consumption was steady for years, but the outlook has now greatly improved because of changes in the population mix (a greater percentage of people of "beer-drinking age"), not because the product has been made to taste so much better that everybody sits around drinking twice as much. The major companies in this industry have grown at a faster rate than the industry by capturing a larger share of the market. The three national brewers —Anheuser-Busch, Pabst, and Schlitz—have consistently increased their market penetration at the expense of the regional firms. This is a difficult kind of growth, with obvious long-term limitations, but given tough, innovative, market-oriented managements, it can be rewarding.

The principal soft-drink manufacturers and distributors have achieved similar impressive results. In the decade ahead, it will be interesting to see how these companies meet the challenge of a population mix that will gradually become less favorable. One successful company in this area—Coca-Cola Bottling of New York —hopes to compensate for a deterioration in demographics by diversifying into different types of soft drinks and by entering the fast-growing wine business, where the population trend has become a plus. (Growing older, the Pepsi generation is becoming the Mogen David generation.)

The more promising industries grow faster than the population. Increased per capita consumption of cosmetics appears to be a reliable fact of life. Women, and men, are using more makeup, more kinds of makeup, more toiletries, more beauty aids and preservatives generally. Similarly, because we appear to be confronted with a relentless increase in the per capita crime rate, the market growth of the protective-service companies is accelerating, in terms of both amount and sophistication of guard service (e.g., the increased use of electronic surveillance). Companies in these industries can grow quite satisfactorily for long periods of time even without increasing their share of the market and without diversifying into other, related fields. For them, crime pays.

When you put good basic industry growth *together* with greater market penetration, the results can be particularly impressive. Avon and Procter & Gamble are solid examples of companies increasing their share in large, rapidly growing markets (cosmetics, toiletries, disposable diapers and other sanitary products).

Let us now observe a few other companies that have created their own markets and where the odds for enduring success for particular products—continued growth of markets over the long term—seem to us somewhat better: Lubrizol, Simplicity Pattern, and Walt Disney.

Beginning with the compounding of special-purpose lubricants in 1928, Lubrizol has used its unique technology to build extraordinary strength in a very specialized field. Today it produces over eight hundred additives and chemical formulations, most of which are custom-prepared for particular requirements. It has worked closely not only with its customers—primarily petroleum refiners and blenders—but with the end-product manufacturers—automotive and off-road equipment manufacturers such as Caterpillar Tractor, Deere, and International Harvester—in developing lubricant and fuel additives to meet new requirements and specifications.

Simplicity Pattern has made itself the dominant company in a $2-billion industry—the home sewing industry.

Of the more than 300 million garments made at home in 1970, Simplicity's patterns were used to make more than half. Simplicity markets patterns for all ages and all degrees of sewing talent. It publishes several magazines that aid in the promotion of its patterns—magazines relating to the latest fashions, instructional texts, teaching guides, and a monthly news bulletin. Twice yearly it publishes a catalogue. Because this company saw a consumer need and created a unique market, it now earns more than 20 percent on shareholders' equity and 12.7 percent on sales after taxes.

Walt Disney, too, is a company that has uniquely created its own markets. Beginning as a producer of animated motion picture shorts in 1923, Disney has considerably expanded its entertainment horizons—for many years with a growing variety of films and then in 1955 with Disneyland, in Anaheim, California. At first the company provided only certain support services at Disneyland, but in 1966 it took over all leased concessions, including those involving the sale of merchandise, and by adroit management succeeded in dramatically improving its profit margins.

Building on the experience gained at Disneyland, in 1971 the company opened Walt Disney World in Orlando, Florida. The original investment in Walt Disney World will exceed $250 million, eclipsing the $17 million originally invested in Disneyland. Walt Disney World owns 27,500 acres, compared with 351 acres in Anaheim. The company intends to develop and reap profits on various real estate holdings surrounding the entertainment complex itself (the initial $250-million project encompasses only 10 percent of the land held by Disney).

It is possible, of course, that these optimistic expectations will not materialize. Perhaps attendance will fall short of forecast. Perhaps unforeseen labor difficulties will arise, increasing costs in unexpected ways. The track record of the Disney organization, however, is extraordinarily good, and the concept is bold. If expectations *are* met, the growth of the organization will be self-sustaining for many years. And the company will have evolved, in a classic way, from *product* to *system*.

We have reviewed in the last two chapters different forms of *innovation* and varied stimuli for market growth. We have shown by a variety of cases how the two forces can work together, in the hands of able managements, to create consistent, rapid sales and earnings advances. Not all markets offer enduring growth. Not all companies understand this fact.

How can one protect oneself against the flash in the pan—the company that shoots its bolt with a single product, or the market that rapidly becomes saturated with competitive products? Will "double-knit" fabrics—so popular at the moment—have a lasting appeal? Will the companies making the machines that make these fabrics—Texfi Industries and Edmos—continue to move ahead? Or is this a specialized, one-shot opportunity, dependent on the whim of the fashion market and not protected by solid, continuous corporate innovation?

As investors we frequently forget that few specific markets grow at an above-average rate forever. Not only do investors lose sight of this and allow their enthusiasm to carry stocks to excessive heights, but corporations are often guilty of nearsightedness, too. Twice, in fifteen years, the television industry has fallen prey to its own enthusiasm and overexpanded its productive capacity.

In order to determine when a new industry or company is getting tired, *keep your eye on product prices*. They will alert you to the fact that an innovation is being converted into a commodity. As this happens, the successful company is transformed, usually with considerable agony for its shareholders, into a problem company. To elaborate:

Stage one: When an innovation is first marketed, the producer sells it at a price that depends almost entirely on the desire of the consumer to have it. Color TV certainly was a great advancement over black and white. RCA, with the only color tube, was in a remarkable position to capitalize on a product that the public was anxious to buy and would pay a premium price to obtain. At this joyous stage in a company's development, prices do not bear any conventional relationship to cost. They are not set by what the competition charges—because there isn't any. And RCA's earnings made a quantum leap.

Stage two: In a genuine effort to broaden the market, the producer cuts prices. He is still not motivated (primarily) by competition. His costs are coming down because of big production runs and improved product yield, and he wants to bring the product into the price range of the next group of consumers, where price holds back the customers.

Stage three: Enter the competition, domestic or foreign. Price-cutting develops as each producer endeavors to increase or hold his market share. We refer to this disease as "shareitis." For many years the aluminum industry has dissipated its volume growth in disastrous battles for market share. The companies involved systematically refer to this struggle as an effort to "broaden the market," but what they are doing is beating each other's brains out. These companies are selling commodities, and they are problem companies.

A more recent, and controversial, change in the price structure of an industry has taken place in the computer field. In 1970 IBM cut prices on certain parts of its line—not, in our judgment, to expand the market but to protect market share. Growth in this industry is clearly slowing down. Parts of the product line—the main frame of computers—no longer have the same powerful innovative features as before; they are more like commodities. The major area of innovation, for the time being, appears to be in peripheral equipment, and the implications of these changes could be profound.

There are two other useful ways (none is foolproof) of determining whether a market for a specific product or company is losing its zing. First, watch to see whether the company in question is diversifying into other markets via acquisitions. Ask yourself why it is doing so if its basic business is so attractive.

The conglomerate phenomenon of the late sixties reflected, more often than not, the piling of weakness on weakness, rather than the addition of strength to strength. The successful programs of growth through acquisition—as in the case of ITT or Textron— are few and far between. We are reminded of Oscar Wilde's observation that "The one charm of marriage is that it makes a life of deception absolutely necessary for both parties."

Second, keep your eye on the importance of replacement business to an industry's or company's overall expansion. Originally, automobiles and television sets were sold to people who had never owned these products before. Today, far more than half of the sales of these items are made to households that have them and are replacing them with newer or better models. There is no reason why a company cannot continue to be successful under these conditions, but growth is almost certainly less dynamic than in the early phases of the industry's development. The key to its success will be its ability profitably to make obsolete its own products. In short, to innovate.

General Motors has done a brilliant job in outmoding its own products. But the automobile industry today is mature, the growth rate for new cars (original equipment) closely tied to population trends, and more interesting opportunities lie in the replacement-parts business and with companies like Genuine Parts.

Until recently, computers were sold or leased almost entirely to customers who had not previously used them. It remains to be seen whether IBM can be as successful in making its own product obsolete and making its own customers trade up, without experiencing too severe inroads from both original-equipment competitors and/or some of the "play-to-play" peripheral equipment suppliers.

To summarize briefly:

In attempting to measure the future growth of a company's market, study whether it is related to:

- Growth in population; and if so, whether you can find interesting situations by picking companies that serve segments of the population growing faster than the population as a whole (because of age or location).
- Growth in per capita consumption (as in wine, cosmetics, drugs).
- Growth in market share.
- Growth because the goods and services are new (Walt Disney, Polaroid), creating new kinds of markets that previously did not exist (this is the most explosive kind).

To spot trouble, keep your eye on:

- Price-cutting. Is it expanding markets or simply cutting profits?
- Diversification efforts. Do they mean that fundamentals in the company's main business are deteriorating?
- Replacement demand in relation to the demand for new equipment. As replacement companies move into large markets, they often create new investment opportunities; they suggest that growth for original-equipment companies has lost its steam.

This brings us to the third characteristic shared by successful companies, one that has a real bearing on the marketing problems we have been discussing:

It is difficult to break into their businesses. Just how difficult depends upon the quality of a successful company's innovational effort. A company that receives a patent or a series of patents for its innovations clearly carves out a degree of protection against competition. However, in many instances it is not the patent alone, but the prolonged development of a series of products (a "system," if you will), a brand name, a body of experience in marketing or in manufacturing, that maintains corporate leadership in the marketplace.

Tampax is a good case in point. No patents have prevented major competitors from entering the market with almost exact replicas of this form of female sanitary protection. However, the strong identification of the brand name Tampax with the company's product has enabled it to dominate the market. This worldwide interchangeability of the brand name Tampax with the product, tampons, has been accompanied by an unusually effective manufacturing effort which has made it impossible for theoretically powerful competitors like Scott Paper Company and Kimberly-Clark to undercut Tampax's prices.

Polaroid, on the other hand, has used its patent position to protect its singular role in the field of instant photography. Despite the expiration of the initial black-and-white patents, a continuing stream of overlapping patents on black-and-white and color photography has preserved Polaroid's market in instant photography intact. While Polaroid believes that its patent position is an essential ingredient in protecting its position, it would also argue that the extreme complexity of its manufacturing process offers important additional protection. Although Eastman Kodak has announced its intention of entering the instant-photography market in the next few years, no one knows yet if this will be done by means of a licensing arrangement with Polaroid or through extended internal efforts of its own. Meanwhile, as indicated earlier, Polaroid has in its laboratories entirely new systems for taking instant color pictures incorporating new color negative processes and new cameras. It intends to ensure its leadership in this market through technological innovation and gradual, planned product obsolescence.

The drug industry has taken conspicuous advantage of patent protection. Sometimes this protected environment has provided an umbrella for further research. Sometimes, however, it has hidden underlying decay. Smith, Kline & French was one of the early leaders in ethical-drug research. It also developed an effective drug-retail force. Protected by worldwide patents on Thorazene, the company's research effort stagnated for many years—too long to offer a cushion against new competition from new ethical-drug products when these patents expired in 1970. Although the company's return on investment remains high, its growth has faltered and the price of its stock dropped sharply.

Innovation is the key. Continuous innovation tends to reinforce patent protection with still more patent protection, with the invaluable protection of manufacturing and marketing know-how, and with the ability to build product and merchandising systems that can most effectively be modified or replaced from *within*—and only with enormous expense and difficulty from *without*—that is, by competitors.

We turn now to two other important ingredients of corporate success that have less to do with innovation than with discipline.

6

The Ingredients of Corporate Success: The Power of Financial Discipline

A FOURTH important characteristic of the successful company is *its ability to control costs*. Securities markets are littered with concerns whose earnings and stock prices collapsed in the late sixties, not because they failed to innovate or to serve growing markets in an effective way, but because they failed to keep the lid on their expenses.

Inflation is, to some extent, both cause and effect where climbing costs are concerned. Debate rages as to which comes first: higher prices, which make higher wages inescapable; or higher wages, which make higher prices inescapable. In any event, the pressure on corporate managements to provide higher wages and more generous fringe benefits has been fierce, especially in a period in which employees were losing ground in real terms.* The impact of succumbing to these pressures when demand for the corporation's goods and services falters—when excess demand is "squeezed out" of the economy, as in 1970—is devastating: profit margins disintegrate.

In some cases corporations have been unable to resist pressures for very substantial increases in employee wages and benefits because of the power of organized labor. Metropolitan daily news-

* That is, their wages were going up less fast than the cost of living.

papers are dramatic cases in point. Many have gone out of business or been absorbed by chains during the last decade, in large measure because of labor demands that could not be soundly accepted. The existence, in a given corporate or industry situation, of unions that can be described as "militant" by any rational yardstick (manifesting a willingness to drive a corporation out of business rather than settle for "less") ought to be considered a fundamental investment deterrent.

In other cases corporations have given in to labor demands that they believed unreasonable—and demands in excess of gains in worker productivity are usually unreasonable—because they believed they could pass on the increases in the form of virtually automatic price increases or could offset them by large capital investments. These expectations have not always been fulfilled. A classic example is the steel industry, where domestic political pressure and surging imports have slowed the rate of price increases and where capital investments have proven inadequate to offset higher costs.

In still other cases managements have let costs—payroll and other operating expenses—get out of hand because they weren't paying sufficient attention to them. The kinds of managements that are "marketing" oriented, that is, concerned with the development of new products and new markets, are sometimes deficient in "minding the shop," in paying attention to the thousands of small managerial details that help keep operating costs under control. As Cervantes once wrote, "It is one thing to praise discipline, and another to submit to it."

Other managements have been mesmerized by their ability to keep earnings moving ahead through the process of acquisitions. These earnings gains have frequently resulted from the methods used to finance and account for these corporate marriages (the use of leverage and "pooling") and not from genuine economies. The managers of the conglomerates have found, repeatedly, that the companies acquired suffer from operating problems no less acute than their own. (Ling-Temco is a leading example.) These problems require an immense amount of postmerger attention. And that attention has not always been forthcoming, as in the case of Penn

Central. Dexterous in conceiving and arranging the mergers, these men have seldom been effective at the mundane job of running the shop (Textron and ITT, once again, are brilliant exceptions).

Finally, some managements have been profligate. We have all read with awe, and probably some envy, of dazzling new executive suites, corporate jets, and elaborate new communications and training programs. Remember National Student Marketing, which leased about 31,000 square feet of office space on Park Avenue at $16–$17 per square foot and six months later was broke? Remember those magnificent, glossy Litton Industries annual reports with pictures of the Parthenon and stirring declarations in behalf of the enduring creativity of Man?

Failure to control costs is not simply a question of inadequate response to pressure for higher wages or of indifference or carelessness; it sometimes results from failure to use effectively the most up-to-date tools that are at hand. A number of companies have given lip service to the computer as a managerial device but not utilized it effectively. Others have neglected to modernize accounting and reporting systems so that they could tell where their costs were, could forecast future costs effectively, spot variations from forecasts promptly, *and then do something about them.*

As an investor you should ask yourself whether costs are really under management's control, or whether a combination of high direct labor costs and union power puts them largely outside management's control. To what extent can the company improve efficiency through capital investment? Has it done so? Are its inventories going up faster than its sales? (This sometimes helps reduce costs over the short run; companies reduce their unit costs by producing in larger quantities, but when the larger quantities do not sell, all hell breaks loose in the form of write-offs.) While not limited to inventory, many huge, extraordinary write-offs which have been reported recently by large companies like Du Pont, General Foods, RCA, and United Aircraft represent belated recognition—by repentant management and boards of directors—of unwise, undisciplined investment decisions in the 1960s.

Are the company's financial statements riddled with footnotes, indicating that it is changing the way it treats its pension costs, or that it is not charging against current sales the "start-up costs" of a new venture, or that it is lengthening the periods in which it depreciates its fixed assets? Often, not always, these are danger signals indicating that costs are not under control, that profit margins are under pressure, and that accounting gimmickry is being brought to the rescue to obscure true results.

The final distinguishing characteristic of the successful company is: *It has financial resources adequate for its growth.*

The company in the best financial condition is the one that generates all the money it needs from internal sources—from retained earnings, from depreciation, and from cash on hand.

Next best is the company that generates most of its money requirements internally and raises the rest from judicious long-term borrowings at favorable rates.

Finally, there is the company that has used up its borrowing power and that must issue preferred stock, various types of securities convertible into common stock, or common stock itself in order to exploit to the full the growth potentials created by its other resources.

The higher the return on invested capital earned by a company, the more likely it is to be able to finance its growth without borrowing or selling more common stock.

Compare the debt-to-equity ratio of the growth companies, shown in the table on page 63, with the same statistics for a group of the best-known conglomerates, shown in the table on page 64. The differences are obvious. Earning an adequate or above-adequate rate of return, the growth companies have low debt-to-equity ratios, and have been reducing their debt ratios. The position of the conglomerates could not be more different.

The market break of 1969–1970 was caused, or accentuated, as much by corporate inattention to "adequate financial resources" as by any other single element. Too casual regard for this fundamental corporate ingredient led to the "liquidity" crisis, epitomized by the bankruptcy of the Penn Central, the commercial paper panic

Growth Companies

	Total Debt Outstanding* (In thousands)			Total Debt as % of Total Capitalization		
	1968	1969	1970	1968	1969	1970
Avon Products	$ 33,201[a]	$ 37,976[a]	$ 39,317	14.1	13.9	12.5
Fort Howard Paper	NA	NA	3,050	NA	NA	4.9
IBM	643,290	677,073	715,091	12.3	11.4	10.7
Johnson & Johnson	31,303	53,377[a]	52,616	8.5	10.0	8.9
Lubrizol	10,672	8,240	5,989	11.8	8.1	5.2
McDonald's	57,257[a]	73,410[a]	90,153	60.0	59.0	45.4
3M	21,778	39,324	71,592	2.4	3.8	6.2
Polaroid	—	—	—	—	—	—
Tampax	—	—	—	—	—	—

* Included in total debt calculations were: long-term debts, convertible subordinated debentures, reserves, deferrals, long-term loans, lease obligations, and certificates of extra compensation. Minority interest and shareholders' equity figures were added to total debt figures to compute total capitalization.
[a] Figures restated to reflect revisions in updated annual reports.

Conglomerates

	Total Debt Outstanding* (In thousands)			Total Debt as % of Total Capitalization		
	1968	1969	1970	1968	1969	1970
Gulf & Western	$ 996,005[a]	$1,062,212	$1,020,253	63	62	62
Ling-Temco-Vought	1,295,344[a]	1,607,231	1,505,608	67	77	80
Litton Industries	292,823[a]	408,638	613,228	32	37	44
Teledyne	172,441[a]	227,193	229,902	32	30	28
Whittaker Corp.	99,263[a]	179,023[a]	188,460	44	51	53

* Included in total debt calculations were all long-term debts, convertible subordinated debentures, reserves, deferrals and accrued pension benefits, where available. Minority interest and shareholders' equity figures were added to total debt figures to compute total capitalization.
[a] Figures restated to reflect revisions in updated annual reports.

that hit Chrysler and the Commercial Credit Corporation, and the demise of some of the oldest brokerage firms in the securities industry.

The problems of the American Telephone & Telegraph Company are, in great part, the result of inadequate financial planning. Today this company has almost exhausted the market for straight debt and straight equity financing and has had to resort to convertible preferred stock financing, the use of warrants and private placements. This pattern is a common one, not only among telephone companies but among most other communications and electric and gas utilities. The need to finance externally is so huge and therefore expensive that the prices of their common stocks are languishing.

If a company *does* have to sell common stock, then the higher the price-earnings ratio at which its stock sells, the fewer shares it will have to issue in order to raise a given sum of money. The following comparison illustrates this basic point:

1. Company A is earning $1 million after taxes. It has 1 million shares outstanding. Earnings per share, therefore, are $1. Its stock sells for 10, or at a price-earnings ratio of 10. The company must raise $10 million in the form of additional stock. To do so with its stock selling at 10, it must issue an additional 1 million shares. After it has issued these shares (and before it has put the money to work), its per share earnings will have dropped to 50 cents.

2. Company B has the same earnings, the same number of shares outstanding, and the same financial requirement. But its stock is selling for $50, or at 50 times current earnings. To raise $10 million, it need issue only 200,000 additional shares (assuming that it, too, can sell them at the current market price). After the issuance of these shares, its earnings will have dropped to 83 cents per share, a decline of only 17 percent compared to 50 percent for Company A.

Polaroid provides a concrete illustration of a company that anticipated its financial needs and took astute advantage of a high price-earnings ratio to raise capital at minimum cost to existing shareholders. Early in 1969, looking ahead to its vast three-year expenditure program, having studied the rising level of interest rates, observing the price of its stock relative to earnings, it determined that a common stock issue was the most assured way of raising the necessary funds. With the shares selling at more than 50 times the latest twelve months' earnings, the company raised almost $100 million through a rights offering of common stock to its shareholders. The equity dilution amounted to 2.7 percent. A year later, when the price of the stock declined by almost 50 percent, it would have cost the company twice as much to raise the same sum. But it had its funds on hand and was able to ride through the market storm unconcerned about its financial resources.

More on this important subject—from a slightly different point of view—in the next chapter.

To summarize what we have been talking about in the last three chapters, the successful company should:

1. Innovate.

2. Serve large and growing markets. (The more effectively it innovates, the more successfully it will create its own markets and sustain its growth.)

3. Serve markets in a manner that makes it difficult for newcomers to enter the field. (Again, this depends on the sophistication and durability of its innovational efforts.)

4. Manage its costs effectively.

5. Have access to sufficient financial resources to exploit the opportunities presented by the combination of factors just listed.

In establishing criteria for success, we have made no reference to the size of a company's research efforts, as a number of other books on this subject do. It is impossible to measure the effectiveness of research in this manner. One company may spend millions on research but scatter its shots ineffectually across a number of uninteresting technologies. Another company may spend less but benefit from the creativity of an inspired individual. The results are highly unpredictable. As Dr. Pierre Rinfret, President and Chief Executive Officer of Rinfret-Boston Associates, has put it, "Research is planned chaos."

In the previous chapter, we emphasized talented management as a crucial element in a company's destiny. There is no way for you as a layman to recognize talented management *except through an analysis of the above five factors.* If you could call directly on Dr. Edwin Land in his laboratory at Polaroid in Cambridge, or Peter McCollough of Xerox, or James Roche of General Motors, and could spend several hours discussing corporate strategy with these men, you might be in a position to analyze for yourself the professional competence and creative flair (or lack thereof) with which these enterprises are managed. You could ask what techniques the company uses to attract outstanding young men, how it trains and motivates them, and how it plans for the future in an uncertain world. These are important questions. But we assume you are *not* in a position to ask them. And too many people who are—too many security analysts—fail to ask them when they should, so that often a brokerage house report contains a great deal of routine descriptive statistical material but very little food for thought with respect to management technique and philosophy. So concentrate on the five ingredients we've discussed above. If you find a company with all five (and don't settle for less) you'll have found superior management as well.

7

The Manifestations of Corporate Success: Consistent Growth and High Return

D URING the sixties, many industries and companies skyrocketed to stock market greatness, only to plummet to earth. The airlines, color television, and electronic components companies are prize examples of short-term success. Some entities in these fields have recovered (at least for a while), others will not be heard from again.

The introduction of the jet engine in the late fifties provided a one-shot burst of prosperity for the airline industry. Color television produced dramatic results for RCA, and then for all the other major members of the industry, as long as color television was a novelty and the market remained unsaturated. But that burst of energy is spent.

We believe that to deserve the characterization, the "successful" company must increase its profits at an above-average rate for a number of years, and should earn an above-average rate of return on its invested capital. There should be a *reasonable* probability that such a company can sustain this predictable earnings growth for a number of years into the future.

For the long-term investor, the key ingredients are *consistency* and *predictability*. No matter how high the return on invested capital may be in any one year, if circumstances prevent a company from sustaining that return for many years ahead, the company will not produce consistent and future gains in earnings per share. Its stock price will ultimately suffer, and probably devastatingly so, when its growth rate deteriorates.

Just as you, the investor, want to earn as high a return as possible on your investment in a stock, so a business enterprise must strive to earn as much money as it possibly can on the money that has been invested in the business by shareholders and lenders.

No greater example exists of a group that has been unsuccessful in producing a decent return on invested capital—despite long-term product growth—than the United States aluminum industry. Gains in worldwide product demand have been extraordinary, as indicated in the table below:

Free World Aluminum Consumption *1961–1971 (in thousands of short tons)*

	Consumption 1961	Consumption 1971	10-Yr. Avg. Annual Growth Rate
United States	1,980.2	3,735.4	8.3%
Total America	2,162.3	4,137.2	8.4
Europe	1,285.2	2,868.1	7.2
Australia and Oceania	26.9	131.3	12.4
Asia	242.9	1,197.0	20.2
Africa	13.7	79.8	18.5
Total Free World	3,731.0	8,413.4	9.1

Source: American Bureau of Metal Statistics.

Not bad product growth! But look what happened to the companies during this period, and what happened to their shares:

Return on Invested Capital* *Four Major Aluminum Companies, 1970 vs. 1955*

	Alcoa	Alcan	Reynolds Metals	Kaiser Aluminum
1955	11.9%	8.3%	12.2%	10.5%
1960	4.8	6.0	5.4	6.1
1970	7.9	8.3	6.3	7.7

* Based on net income plus interest as percent of average invested capital.

During the sixteen-year period these companies generated insignificant growth in per share earnings:

Earnings per Share of Four Major Aluminum Companies vs. Dow Jones Industrials

	Alcoa	Alcan	Reynolds Metals	Kaiser Aluminum	DJII
1955	$4.20	$1.59*	$2.24	$2.86	$35.78
1960	1.76	1.30	1.27	1.17	32.21
1970	5.20	2.08	2.51	2.50	51.02

In Canadian dollars.

Not one of these major companies was able to translate superior volume growth into earnings growth equivalent to that of the Dow Jones Industrials over a sixteen-year span. Time enough to provide great disillusionment to investors in aluminum stocks.

End-of-Year Closing Share Price for Four Major Aluminum Companies

	Alcoa	Alcan	Reynolds Metals	Kaiser Aluminum
1955	88	35	51	41
1960	69	32	47	41
1970	57	23	27	35

In their infatuation with growth, most analysts fail to pay sufficient attention to the quality of a company's earning power. They are like the beauty contest judges who focus on the contestant's thirty-eight-inch bosom, failing to see her thirty-eight-inch waist. The judge may have a perfectly pleasant time, but he or she isn't going to pick many real winners. This was the real meaning of the conglomerate mania of the late sixties. Everyone kept his eye on the growth rate, but few analyzed the flabby underpinnings that ultimately proved the downfall of innumerable companies.

By the "quality" of profits we refer not merely, or necessarily, to high profits in relation to sales (high profit margins) but to a sound return on invested capital. Alfred Sloan of General Motors said it many years ago: "The fundamental concern of a business is to earn a return on its capital."

What do we mean by "above-average" rates of growth and rates of return, and how many companies have been able to make a satisfactory showing? As we discussed earlier (see Chapter 2), satisfactory growth rates for common stocks at a given time depend on the prevailing level of interest rates. What was attractive when prime rates were 4 percent and inflation 1 percent may be unattractive with prime interest rates at 6 percent and inflation raging at over 5 percent.

The following tables may serve as guidelines for now:

Annual per Share Earnings Growth	Our Rating
Less than 4%	Below average
4 to 5%	Average
5 to 7%	Above average
7 to 10%	Very good
10 to 15%	Unusual (excellent)
15% or more	Rare (superlative)

Annual After-tax Return on Invested Capital	Our Rating
Less than 10%	Below average
10 to 12%	Average
12 to 15%	Above average
15 to 20%	Remarkable
20% or more	Spectacular

The two tables above are inextricably linked. If a company earns a return of 10 percent on its capital and pays out 50 percent of it to shareholders as a common stock dividend, it will retain the remaining 50 percent, which is the equivalent of a 5 percent return —adding 5 percent to its capital base. All other things being equal, it should be able to use this additional capital to support a growth in its business of 5 percent. (In fact, there are a great many variables that enter the equation, but on a hypothetical basis the analysis is sound.)

Carrying this further, you can see that a company which earns 20 percent on its capital theoretically can pay out 50 percent of its earnings and support a 10 percent rate of growth. Or it can retain all 20 percent in the business and support a 20 percent rate of growth. This explains why rapidly growing companies prefer to pay only a minute percentage of their earnings as dividends. They can utilize "retained earnings" more effectively to keep growing. It also explains why companies with high rates of return can finance rapid growth more soundly than those with low returns. The latter must borrow to grow; the former often need not.

With growth in the use of computers, most of the advisory services (such as Standard & Poor's and Moody's) have been able to provide timely and useful data on rates of growth and rates of return. *Fortune* magazine annually presents detailed data of this sort for the largest business enterprises in the United States and abroad. *Forbes* has helpful information, too. But in the final analysis your broker or investment adviser will have to help you to judge the underlying quality of the figures in question.

A high return on capital can sometimes create problems. In the utilities—electric, gas, telephone, and water—regulatory bodies impose strict limitations on the amount companies can earn on their investment. In the transportation industry the Interstate Commerce Commission spells out what each segment of the industry should charge for fares or rates, which is, in effect, a controlling element—a ceiling on rate of return. In other industries (drugs, for example) high returns occasionally raise the threat of governmental intervention. In recent years, however, most companies have had the problem of low, not high, returns.

Throughout this book we have referred to the element of consistency and predictability in a corporation's earnings. The ability to show earnings increments year after year, regardless of economic circumstances, is an integral characteristic of the truly successful company. The more years that a company demonstrates its ability to sustain rising earnings, the greater the market's confidence in this investment.

Which companies have done the best job—in terms of providing consistent growth and reasonable rates of return—during the last decade? To discover this, we have studied more than 1,700 companies to find those with the following records of accomplishment:

1. Average annual earnings per share growth of at least 12 percent during the ten-year period 1960–1970 and the five-year period 1965–1970.

2. An earnings increase in *every* year of the decade.

3. An average annual return on total invested capital of 12 percent for both the 1960–1970 and 1965–1970 periods.

Only 30 companies out of the more than 1,700 U.S. corporations meet all these specifications. They are listed in the table on pages 74–75.

While growth rates and returns sometimes dropped in the second half of the decade, they were still remarkably good. And a number of companies, such as Simplicity Pattern, Baxter Laboratories, Johnson & Johnson, and Philip Morris, improved their compound earnings growth and their return on capital during the last half of the decade.

With the exception of IBM, Perkin-Elmer, Xerox, and three oil and gas producers, the firms that made the list were either *consumer*- or *service*-related companies, or provided a product or a service of a disposable nature. Only Perkin-Elmer can be considered to have been exclusively in a high-technology business with a predominantly government-oriented sales base. Very few other technologically oriented companies, except Xerox and IBM, met our growth standards during the last decade. The predominance of consumer- and service-oriented companies is dramatic and symptomatic.

A number of other fundamental themes are suggested by this table: (1) Many of these companies are characterized by a sim-

Companies with Consistent Growth *1960–1970*

Company	Annual Growth in EPS* 1960–1970	1965–1970	Closing Price 1960 vs. 1970
Xerox	46.1%	20.2%	$ 4.9— 86.5
Holiday Inns	36.4	37.7	2.6— 38.5
Masco Corporation	24.2	12.3	0.7— 46.0
Dr. Pepper	24.1	17.5	1.2— 23.0
Texas Oil & Gas	23.0	16.1	3.2— 29.3
Emery Air Freight	22.0	15.4	5.7— 57.8
Simplicity Pattern	21.7	22.6	7.8— 95.8
Crown Cork & Seal	21.0	11.9†	2.2— 18.1
Baxter Laboratories	20.9	23.2	3.3— 25.9
Marriott	20.5	17.1	3.6— 28.7
Economic Laboratory	19.4	18.7	1.7— 23.8
Avon Products	19.2	15.5	13.2— 88.5
Int'l Flavors & Fragrances	19.2	13.6	NA— 64.8
Weis Markets	18.2	12.6	NA— 38.0
Gen. Am. Oil of Texas	18.2	17.0	14.9— 38.4
Perkin-Elmer	18.1	15.4	12.2— 31.5
Lubrizol	18.0	17.3	4.6— 75.4
Johnson & Johnson	17.7	20.2	8.3— 57.0
Bristol-Myers	17.3	12.5	16.3— 64.0
ARA Services	17.2	12.2	31.0—119.3
Tampax	16.7	13.5	54.3—207.0
IBM	16.5	17.0	102.9—317.8
Carnation	16.5	15.1	12.8— 74.6
Heublein	15.5	12.8	5.8— 46.0
Philip Morris	14.4	21.6	13.3— 49.5
Coca-Cola	13.8	12.5	20.1— 84.8
Schering	13.7	16.3	13.9— 62.8
Emerson Electric	13.6	13.6	12.2— 66.0
Petrolane	13.5	17.7	16.1— 36.8
ITT	12.9	12.3	24.0— 50.6

Source: Investors Management Sciences, Inc., a subsidiary of Standard & Poor's Corporation; compilation courtesy of Merrill, Lynch, Pierce, Fenner & Smith, Inc.
* *Computed on a log-linear basis.*
† *These companies narrowly miss meeting the tests we have set; we've cheated a little by including them. Their records are superb, much better than the next closest contenders.*

Percent Change in Price 1960–1970	Average Return on Invested Capital		Average Price-Earnings Ratio 1960 vs. 1970
	1960–1970	1965–1970	
1653.4	22.8%	22.6%	75.4—37.7X
1397.6	12.3	13.9	38.8—24.1
1122.8	24.7	30.1	18.2—32.4
1755.5	22.5	28.3	13.8—30.7
819.6	15.2	11.6†	21.3—27.4
921.0	53.0	49.6	36.7—34.6
1122.8	24.7	26.3	18.2—32.4
740.6	12.5	14.1	11.6— 12.3
696.2	13.7	14.4	30.9—52.9
696.8	14.3	14.1	22.0—34.3
1334.4	18.2	20.3	12.9—38.1
570.0	40.8	42.0	35.5—42.9
NA	21.3	24.8	NA—43.9
NA	23.5	23.2	NA—11.6
157.0	12.0	12.2	32.8—10.6
159.1	11.9†	12.3	37.7—26.1
1534.6	19.8	22.0	10.4—27.0
586.3	12.8	15.7	25.2—32.1
292.3	23.4	24.7	25.6—25.4
284.7	13.0	12.5	32.1—27.7
281.0	41.4	39.7	30.9—28.4
208.9	18.2	19.0	45.1—34.0
481.6	12.7	14.6	11.3—16.7
692.1	19.5	22.1	11.5—26.7
271.3	12.4	14.9	13.0—11.6
321.8	16.8	NA	22.5—30.3
350.2	15.6	NA	26.3—28.8
442.5	19.5	20.4	15.2—23.8
128.1	16.0	15.8	19.6—12.2
110.9	11.9	13.8	20.7—14.3

plicity and directness, both in their concepts of business and in their capitalizations, which stand in contrast to the convoluted product lines and capital structures of so many acquisitive companies that strove and failed to succeed in the sixties. (2) Many of the concerns have developed specialty products or services, pyramiding *related* new products and services upon small sales bases. (3) Many of them have been successful in developing products that are disposable or that lend themselves to planned obsolescence. (4) Many have been able to increase market shares against competition and to sustain profit margins through careful control of costs. (5) Many are worldwide. In 1970, for example, IBM's overseas earnings exceeded domestic profits, and Lubrizol's international sales amounted to almost 60 percent of its total revenues.

Only one company on this list had sales of more than $1 billion at the beginning of the period. Interestingly, only five that qualify in terms of growth rate and return on capital in our list are on the list of the fifty favorite holdings of the mutual funds as reported by *Vickers:** IBM, Xerox, Philip Morris, Avon Products, and ITT, in that order. These are the corporations whose capitalizations are large enough to permit wide institutional ownership. How many of these companies will still meet our growth specifications five years from now?

Eight additional companies had sales in excess of $100 million in 1960 (five of them had more than $200 million in volume). But the overwhelming number had small sales bases at the start of the period. Twenty of the thirty had sales of less than $100 million. Many of these companies were minute, and only at the inception of dramatic sales and earnings expansions. Sales of Texas Oil & Gas, for example, amounted to only $1.3 million; of Masco, $6.4 million; of Dr. Pepper, $13 million. The majority of companies were in the $20 to $50 million sales range.

From this we confirm the obvious: that the ability to sustain extraordinary growth of the kind we have defined becomes harder as the sales base of a company grows beyond a certain point. But more positively: that there are extraordinary opportunities in small- to moderate-sized concerns that may not yet have entered the institutional consciousness.

While a few of the companies on this list made acquisitions dur-

* Report for period ended March 31, 1971.

ing the decade, in almost all cases the acquisition merely supplemented existing lines (as with ARA Services or Bristol-Myers), helping expand a range of products or services. The only exception to this is ITT. The latter acquired 108 companies in the United States before the Justice Department called a halt. The key to success in the great majority of the other cases was an unswerving and straightforward pursuit of one essential product or service.

Success, as we have defined it, need not be limited to the select group of companies that meet the standards set forth above. In addition, there is a small but impressive group of companies that have either (1) grown consistently for ten or more years at rates ranging from 6 to 11 percent per annum (including such corporate giants as Eastman Kodak, Procter & Gamble, and Minnesota Mining & Manufacturing, and such moderate-sized companies as Genuine Parts and Fischbach & Moore); (2) had one or two troublesome years during the past decade, but have resolved their problems and have eight or nine years of earnings growth out of the last ten, and are now forging ahead (a varied fare, as shown in the table on page 78, ranging from Royal Crown Cola to Delta Air Lines); or (3) whose record of continuous earnings growth covers at least five consecutive years (1965–1970) but not yet ten. Reasons for the shorter span of unbroken progress may vary, from the fact that the companies may not yet have been in business for ten years (or that public documentation is not available that far back) to the explanation that they reordered their business subsequent to 1960, as in the case of Kresge.

We note that as the history of consecutive growth for these companies declines, the breadth and variety of corporate activity widen. The great majority of companies that survived the last decade with only one year of earnings interruption were still oriented closely to the consumer and to disposable products and services. In one manner or another their products were distinctive. Even Delta Air Lines, which outperformed all other airlines, was blessed with a uniquely superior route structure (managerial skills were also integral to its success).

Companies with Nine Years Up Earnings per Share

Company	Annual Growth in EPS* 1960–1970	Closing Price 1960 vs. 1970
Syntex	43.8%	$ 5.2—38.2
Delta Air Lines	30.0	1.9—33.5
Capital Cities Broadcasting	25.1	2.6—29.4
Heileman Brewing	21.9	1.8—24.0
Lucky Stores	21.4	3.7—33.7
Host International	18.4	5.5—28.5
Eli Lilly	16.9	16.8—99.3
AMP	15.7	11.1—57.0
Prentice-Hall	15.4	19.8—44.7
Zale	13.8	4.5—37.0
Merck	13.8	28.2—99.0
Thomas & Betts	12.0	10.3—37.0

Companies with Eight Years Up Earnings per Share

Company	Annual Growth in EPS* 1960–1970	Closing Price 1960 vs. 1970
Gulf & Western Industries	30.6	2.6—19.3
Polaroid	20.7	23.3—77.0
Oshawa Wholesale Ltd.	20.6	1.0— 9.6
Royal Crown Cola	18.8	4.2—16.5
Hewlett-Packard	15.4	14.6—30.0
Clark Equipment	15.3	18.6—36.6
G. D. Searle	15.2	23.1—52.3
Melville Shoe	13.9	7.6—41.0
Halliburton	12.8	10.6—47.4
Caterpillar Tractor	12.6	15.2—42.6
Gardner-Denver	12.0	14.4—36.6
Nalco Chemical	12.0	12.3—42.3

Source: *Investors Management Sciences, Inc., a subsidiary of Standard & Poor's Corporation; compilation courtesy of Merrill, Lynch, Pierce, Fenner & Smith, Inc.*
* *Computed on a log-linear basis.*

When we examine the list of companies that experienced two years of interrupted earnings growth during the decade, we begin to observe the impact of the business cycle. Clark Equipment, Halliburton, Caterpillar Tractor, and Hewlett-Packard are rare companies with essential products and worldwide markets, but as capital equipment producers they feel the impact of the business cycle. During the 1960s their earnings trends reflected one or both of the business adjustments of 1961–1962 and 1966–1967.

Percent Change in Price 1960–1970	Average Return on Invested Capital 1960–1970	Average Price-Earnings Ratio 1960 vs. 1970
627.6	33.3%	163.5—34.6X
1663.2	16.6	10.1—12.9
1030.8	16.0	14.0—17.0
1261.7	16.1	10.0—17.5
801.1	18.1	14.2—16.1
421.3	18.1	21.6—32.7
492.8	19.3	31.1—32.6
412.7	26.4	21.3—25.0
125.3	29.6	46.5—26.4
720.2	17.1	13.6—21.9
250.6	23.5	33.0—29.9
258.2	21.9	18.5—19.1
647.1	17.8	16.9— 6.6X
230.8	23.6	94.0—48.8
860.0	18.3	8.6—24.6
290.8	24.4	23.4—15.4
105.5	19.8	52.3—41.4
96.8	15.4	26.1—10.7
126.1	32.8	35.6—19.1
439.5	18.8	14.6—19.2
347.2	15.1	13.4—15.1
180.3	17.0	19.0—14.7
154.2	17.2	14.3—10.2
242.5	19.4	22.7—37.4

Polaroid illustrates another pattern. Its sales and earnings grow in giant steps. In between there are plateaus. Sales growth tapers off before the introduction of a new generation of products, and earnings feel the impact of massive research outlays. Dr. Edwin L. Land described Polaroid's investment cycle in the 1968 annual report:

Our history over the last 30 years shows a succession of periods in each of which we first invest and then consolidate at a level of income higher than that for the previous period of consolidation. If we are to

The Research Cycle and Polaroid Corporation

	1970	1969	1968	1967
Sales (in thousands)	$444,285	$465,609	$402,070	$374,35
Pre-tax profit margin	25.6%	28.1%	32.1%	30.6%
Research, Development, and Engineering expenditures (in thousands)	$ 58,000	$ 40,600	$ 26,731	$ 21,02
expenditures as % of sales	13.1	8.7	6.6	5.6

* All sales figures exclude unconsolidated foreign sales. Research, Development, and Engineering expenditures as reported are charged against domestic revenues.
† Actual figure not available. Approximate figure is that given in a ten-year bar chart presentation in 1969 Polaroid annual report.

continue our cycle of discovery and expansion, we must prepare for a rigorous new cycle. Because the volume of our activity is so much larger now than it was during our previous cycle, it seems clear to us that no single field, however attractive, should be relied on to take us into the next phase of our growth. Therefore, we came to the conclusion that we should not select from among these major new opportunities, but rather proceed enthusiastically and concurrently with the pursuit of all of them. . . . We also have to take into account the somewhat unpredictable and temporary effect on the growth of earnings of the heavy expenses associated with large capital investment.

The table above illustrates the impact of this cycle on Polaroid's results over the twelve years 1958–1970.

In 1971 Polaroid stayed on its latest plateau. One of the great corporate suspense stories of the seventies revolves around the size and the timing of its next great step forward.

In the case of companies with only five years of continuous earnings improvement, you should begin to question the difference between substantive progress and surface growth. Witness the divergent realities of McDonald's Corporation and Denny's Restaurants. Within the food franchise field, these two companies typify the difference between real success and apparent success. Both had excellent reported results for the years under review, but Denny's managerial practices were not sound enough to withstand either the recession of 1970 or a required switch to more conservative accounting procedures.

)66	1965	1964	1963	1962	1961	1960	1959	1958
5,551	$202,228	$138,077	$122,333	$102,589	$100,562	$98,734	$89,487	$65,271
9.1%	28.4%	25.8%	19.8%	21.1%	17.4%	19.5%	26.2%	24.5%
,594	$ 13,000*	$ 9,098	$ 8,011	$ 9,456	$ 6,670	$ 6,209	$ 4,551	$ 2,982
1.9	6.4†	6.6	6.5	9.2	6.6	6.3	5.1	4.6

Shares of the companies that showed *unbroken* earnings increases for the entire decade (the ones shown in the table on pages 74–75) had an average price appreciation during the period of 683.3 percent; the stocks of companies that had one year of growth interruption during this period experienced an average increase of 672.1 percent; however, when a company's earnings growth was interrupted twice, whether in consecutive years or not, cumulative market appreciation was much lower (although very good) at 310.1 percent.*

The market today is quick to reward success, as we have defined it, with rapid stock market appreciation. It is just as impulsive in its withdrawal of approval because of earnings deterioration.

What has happened to some of our "blue chips"? Corporate giants such as Du Pont, General Electric, General Motors, International Paper, and Union Carbide have had rough sledding in the market during these years.

Despite their prominence, these companies have faced a variety of obstacles, including slow or erratic market growth, wage-price

* The rate of return we have established as reasonable for you is 10 to 12 percent annually, or 159 percent to 211 percent, over 10 years, much lower than the figures just cited. We believe the lower 10 to 12 percent return is more realistic because: (1) we have identified the stocks described above with the benefit of hindsight; (2) even if this particular group of companies is successful for another ten years, it will provide less growth than in the previous ten because of the limitations of size; (3) even if you *are* successful in picking several companies that do as well as these have, collectively, in the last decade, your batting average will not be perfect. You will make offsetting mistakes that are likely to bring your overall return down to the range we regard as reasonable.

Corporate Giants

	Annual Growth in Earnings per Share*		Return on Capital	
	1960–1970	1965–1970	1960–1970	1965–1970
Du Pont	−3.7%	− 3.9%	16.0%	14.5%
Gen. Electric	4.1	− 2.7	14.5	13.9
Gen. Motors	0.7	−16.7	19.7	16.6
Int'l Paper	4.1	− 0.3	9.0	9.4
Standard Oil of N.J.	6.3	4.4	11.9	12.7
Union Carbide	1.4	− 7.4	10.8	9.4

Source: Investors Management Sciences, Inc., a subsidiary of Standard & Poor's Corporation; compilation courtesy of Merrill, Lynch, Pierce, Fenner & Smith, Inc.
* *Computed on a log-linear basis.*

pressures, and foreign competition. They have been unrewarding investments. Within the period you may have been able to catch several cyclical swings in price, but you have had to be agile.

Let us review our conclusions and add a cautionary note or two.

Not surprisingly, these tables show that performance counts. A company whose shares grow at an above-average rate and earn an above-average return for a number of years is almost sure to be an above-average performer. Although it may take time, its success will be recognized in the marketplace.

The tables suggest that the better a company performs in these three respects—the faster its growth, the more consistent its growth, and the higher its return on capital—the more its stock will go up.

Remarkably few companies can sustain above-average growth for long periods. Too many investors try to concentrate on the spectacular short-term earnings trends, which flicker out with disastrous consequences, while ignoring the 10 to 12 percent year-in, year-out growers. As a result they miss rewarding and straightforward investment opportunities.

We accept the premise that if a company does not meet our statistical criteria, it is not truly successful. It may seem successful to the untrained eye, but somewhere there lurks a flaw. The investment record of the last decade is strewn with the remnants of companies that tried to turn a temporary success, an innovational product or concept, an accounting gimmick, or a series of diverse acquisitions into a prolonged trend. For the most part these were problem companies in a favorable phase. Their success was not enduring.

The fact that such stocks have periodically done well reinforces our belief that there is an occasional place for this type of company in your portfolio—but no room for a major emphasis or long-term holding. You must know when to sell.

It is important that you use these statistical tools with flexibility. There is nothing magical about five- and ten-year periods. We use them because they are reasonable measuring periods for company statistical data. When you study the performances of more than seventeen hundred companies over an identical time span, a few will inevitably take it on the chin because of statistical bad luck. Major mergers or acquisitions distort statistical comparisons. Many fine corporations become public for the first time, and historical data are not accessible. Companies such as Schering-Plough, Squibb, Norton Simon, Amerada Hess, and the Gannett Company are among those affected by these conditions as well as others you undoubtedly discovered yourself. The specific time span we have utilized may coincide with an off year for a major company, such as Eastman Kodak in 1970.

Above all, we stress that these tables describe the past, and not the future. The companies listed may not rank among the outstanding successes of tomorrow. The truly successful performers of the future may today have only brief records of earnings growth. They are emerging successes. If their results gradually produce the kind of records we have been discussing, their stocks will be rewarding.

8

Sweet Sixteen: Fascinating Examples of Enduring Corporate Success

WE have analyzed the five elements that produce enduring corporate success. Now let's look at sixteen companies that embody that success. A few of them we've already mentioned in passing; others are new. We've attempted to select a cross-section of companies: large and small; widely known and relatively obscure; consumer-oriented, industrial, and agricultural. As you read these company descriptions, ask yourself whether the five factors that we insist are an integral part of enduring success are really present. Do the companies innovate? If so, how? Do they operate in large, growing markets? Are their market positions impregnable? Do they exercise financial control? Are they adequately financed? We have selected these companies not because we believe they are all fine investments now (this is not a glorified "tip sheet") but because we believe they are fascinating *models*. Some of them may be attractive investments when you read this book. Others will not. But hopefully they will serve for a long time to come as yardsticks against which to measure a variety of other investment opportunities.

Our observations are based on data accumulated from basic public sources: corporate annual reports and prospectuses; business publications like *Fortune, Forbes, Barron's,* and *Business Week;*

daily newspapers, including the *Wall Street Journal;* and from innumerable research reports prepared by capable security analysts in brokerage houses.

Avon Products, Incorporated

Since 1965 everything about Avon has slightly more than doubled.

Avon Products

	Sales (in millions)	Net Income (in millions)	Earnings per Share	Price Range	Sales Representatives
1970	$760	$99.0	$1.72	92–59	450,000†
1965	$352	$48.0	$ .82	38–26	200,000†
% Change	116	106	110	136*	125

* *Percentage change in price in this and subsequent tables in this chapter is calculated using midpoints of price ranges.*
  † *Approximate.*

The last five years have seen Avon Products successfully enter a number of new overseas markets in Europe, Latin America, and the Far East. Avon entered Japan, the second largest world cosmetics market, in 1969; Argentina, in 1970; and Sweden and Holland, in 1971. Although it takes several years to bring ventures in new nations to a state of profitability and foreign markets are not as profitable as domestic markets, the company's growth abroad is eminently sound, and its progress there is faster than that domestically.

As Avon's sales base and its staff of sales representatives (still mostly housewives functioning on a part-time basis) have grown, its research and marketing people have begun to explore additional products—and marketing concepts. The company is beginning to sell moderately priced costume jewelry through its representatives; it tested a line of greeting cards in 1971 on the same basis; and it is preparing to enter the creative stitchery field. It is now testing six beauty salons in the Denver, Colorado, area to determine if its return on invested capital in that business can approach returns on its existing business. It is exploring the possibilities of entering the home sewing market.

Avon has worked hard to assure the continued effectiveness of the sales techniques that lie at the heart of its business: to increase its sales per representative, it has defined sales territories more precisely; it has changed its selling campaign cycle from three weeks to two; and it has continued to evaluate and upgrade its products (in the last ten years it has added more than two hundred scientists and technicians to the research staff).

While the present size of the company and the price of its shares are awesome to those of us who first looked at Avon years ago, the company's worldwide appeal is still powerful. It provides *real* sales incentives to its representatives, who comprise the largest sales force in the world (now more than 550,000 representatives); it provides *real* convenience to its customers; and it manages its business with precision.

Underlying its continued impressive prospects is the unchanging, and perhaps unchangeable, vanity of the human species. We are all—man, woman, and child—like the peacock in our infatuation with appearance. Avon Products should be able to sustain a 12 to 13 percent growth rate—compared with a predicted 17 to 18 percent five years ago—for some time to come.

DEKALB AgResearch, Inc.

The following research report from a Wall Street investment banking firm* came to our attention in December 1971. The summary caught our eye:

We regard DEKALB AgResearch as an attractive investment. Its business is hybridization. Its products are proprietary. Its markets are world-wide. Growth has been superior. Its business has not been characterized by the wide swings typical of either the commodity or capital

* White, Weld & Company.

equipment companies in the agricultural market. The following are of particular importance:

1. The company is an innovator. Its growth has come from the introduction of new and superior proprietary hybrid seeds and animals developed by its research department. Through the introduction of new hybrids, it has created new markets.

2. Marketing is one of DEKALB's real strengths. Direct calls on farmers are made by the company's large farmer-dealer organization not unlike the Avon Products technique.

3. Its markets are not easy to enter. The development of a marketing and research organization is long and costly. Competition, as a result, is primarily on a quality and performance basis rather than price.

4. The company has a strong balance sheet and adequate financial resources. Foreseeable growth will be financed from internally generated funds.

The company's business is the generation of protein. It does this by developing improved hybrid seeds (primarily corn and sorghum) and animals (primarily chicks for egg production and breeding stock).

Hybrid seeds provide higher yields to farmers. They are also more resistant to disease and other agricultural perils. They cost more, but the incremental return for the user is impressive (in corn it is estimated the farmer gets $10 to $15 back for every extra dollar invested in hybrid seed). Furthermore, hybrids do not replace themselves like normal seeds; thus farmers must buy new hybrid seeds for each new crop, and the business, from DEKALB's standpoint, has a strong built-in "replacement" feature.

More than 75 percent of DEKALB's sales and earnings come from the sale of hybrid *seeds*. About 10 to 15 percent come from the sale of hybrid poultry. The rest comes from a small oil and gas production business, which helps DEKALB to control its earnings progress, through increases or reductions in exploration outlays.

The company is working hard to develop hybrid wheat seeds. No hybrids yet exist in this market, which is larger than DEKALB's largest market today: corn. Whether and when the company will successfully develop this product is difficult to predict. It has been conducting intensive research on the project since 1961, believes it is ahead of others, and that success is in sight. The company's research budget exceeds $4 million. It has a staff of over one hundred scientists (thirty-one Ph.D.s). Work is progressing not only on wheat but on development of new swine-breeding techniques, improved rice and barley, and improvement in existing lines.

DEKALB serves large, important markets with proprietary products. It reaches its major markets—the corn farmer—through a unique sales organization—over 7,000 farmer-dealer salesmen who call on 100 to 150 neighbors each, supplementing their regular incomes, to the tune of $3,000 to $4,000 annually, by spreading the word about, and sales of, DEKALB's line.

DEKALB is not immune to cyclical forces. Its earnings growth may not be as consistent, year to year, as those of other companies we describe. However, we are drawn to the combination of strong technology and unique marketing in a field of fundamental and enduring worldwide importance.

The company has a strong and growing position overseas (more than 20 percent of its total seed sales) and is in solid financial shape.

DEKALB AgResearch, Inc.

	Net Sales (in millions)	Net Income (in millions)	Earnings per Share	Price Range
F 1971*	$123.5	$10.4	$1.87	55–31
F 1966†	$ 56.4	$ 5.8	$1.00	NA
% Change	119	79	87	

Fiscal year ended August 31.
† Fiscal year ended June 30.

Walt Disney Productions

The best-known corporate products in the world—from the United States to Morocco to India to Japan—are those produced by Eastman Kodak, Coca-Cola, and Walt Disney. Virtually everyone who has spent an afternoon or evening at the movies has seen or heard of Mickey Mouse, Donald Duck, and other Disney cartoon characters. Many who have *not* been to the movies have also heard of these colorful figures.

What is the company today? Approximately $85.1 million of its 1970 revenue came from films and related activities. The remaining $82 million came from its recreational facilities.

Disney makes three to five new motion pictures each year, stressing "wholesome entertainment for the family." The company continually rereleases old films, mixing new and old each year in the most profitable way it can. The library of great Disney motion pictures, commencing with *Fantasia,* has a vast intrinsic value not shown on its balance sheet. *None of its feature films considered suitable for continuing worldwide theatrical rereleases has ever been licensed for national television.* Each year this library of films gains in value.

Fifteen years ago Walt Disney's fertile mind conceived the possibility of converting the one-dimensional visual experience of his animated cartoons into three-dimensional enjoyment, and thus Disneyland was born. But the newest Disney enterprise, Walt Disney World in Florida, bears the same relationship to Disneyland as a Boeing 747 to a Toonerville trolley. The investment in Florida is, thus far, more than $250 million versus $17 million in California, and covers 27,500 acres versus 361 acres. More than two dozen major companies have put up substantial sums of money to obtain commercial identification with Walt Disney World. Eastern Airlines, for example, paid $10 million to be able to call itself "The official airline of Walt Disney World" for the next ten years. Other major companies that have paid for the privilege of a Walt Disney World affiliation include Hertz, Coca-Cola, Pepsi-Cola, Sara Lee, Borden, Monsanto, and the Florida Citrus Fruit Commission, to name just a few. Disney has informed all these corporate figures that they should not expect to earn a normal return on these investments but to consider them, at least in part, as advertising and promotional outlays.

The enlargement of the parent company's activities at Walt Disney World would defy the imagination, if imagination were not the key to Walt Disney in the first place. Additional endeavors, all to be owned by Disney, include land development, closed-circuit TV systems, lodging facilities (from camping to luxury hotels), automotive services, printing, insurance, a laundry, convention halls, recreation facilities (golf, boating, fishing, tennis, camping), and general contracting (the Buena Vista Construction Company). There is a boldness here that reminds us of Polaroid, of ITT, of Kresge, and of Xerox in its early days.

Walt Disney himself died in 1966, and his brother Roy, an important figure in the company, died late in 1971 at the age of seventy-eight. The management developed by these two brothers and now headed by Donn B. Tatum is held in high esteem by the financial world.

Disney sells at the highest price-earnings ratio of any company described in this book. If Walt Disney World clicks, investors will understand why.

Walt Disney Productions

	Net Sales (in millions)	Net Income (in millions)	Earnings per Share	Price Range
F 1971*	$175.6	$26.7	$2.07	129–69
F 1966†	$116.5	$12.4	$1.40	19–9
% Change	51	115	48	607

* *Fiscal year ended October 3.*
† *Fiscal year ended October 1.*

Fort Howard Paper Company

Every once in a while a company emerges from the dwindling preserves of private ownership in the United States economy to prove again that within the vastness of the domestic economy there are still surprising ways for creative managements to build distinctive companies with bright futures. The Fort Howard Paper

Company is an enterprise which first revealed its special corporate strengths to public view in 1971.*

Within an industry notable for many difficulties ("shareitis," price-cutting, poor profit margins), the Fort Howard Paper Company has had an outstanding record. Over the last forty years the company has developed remarkable techniques for recycling waste paper of all kinds, from newspapers to old telephone books. Its particular methods for de-inking printed paper and reprocessing it have enabled the company to obtain substantial cost advantages in the production of its paper products. Fort Howard has no commitment to the maintenance of vast forests of raw materials; instead, it has a vast warehouse for the storage of waste papers of all types. Access to waste paper is large; only 20 percent of the available supply of paper in the United States is now recycled for further use (ecological pressures may alter this ratio somewhat in the future). All the company's facilities are located in Green Bay, Wisconsin. Its manufacturing facilities are housed in one interconnecting plant, which may be the world's largest paper-manufacturing facility under one roof. Labor-management relationships are exceptionally cordial and well structured. There is periodic communication between top management and employees at all levels of operations. On each significant anniversary of one's employment (five, ten, fifteen years, etc.) each member of the staff is invited for coffee with the president. Community relations are taken seriously and are excellent.

Such careful attention to detail characterizes all aspects of the business. Fort Howard has maintained 23 to 25 percent pretax profit margins, while its principal competitors do no better than 8 to 9 percent pretax. During the last five years the company has increased its per share earnings 70 percent in a straight line. Its sales have grown at a 12 to 13 percent rate compounded annually. While its larger competitors have been competing aggressively for the consumer market for sanitary papers, Fort Howard has carved

* When Goldman, Sachs underwrote an issue of 432,000 shares at $27.75 each.

a special niche for itself in the commercial and industrial markets for paper towels, napkins, toilet and facial tissues, and specialty products, marketed through more than 2,500 distributors. The company's financial position is just as impressive as its production and marketing strengths. With no funded debt, and enough dollars in the bank to more than match all current liabilities, it is able to obtain advantageous prices by its prompt payment for its raw material supplies of waste paper, coal (for its own power plant), and pulp, all of which it stocks in heavy quantities.

Fort Howard is the epitome of the strong, insular, and independent American family-built corporation. When we talked to the president of the company about some of the monetary problems facing the world, he remarked, "Well, here in Green Bay we worry more about the Packers than about world financial problems!"

In 1972 the company should come close to $100 million in sales volume, and its present expansion program should permit it to surpass that level easily shortly thereafter. Our conclusion is that this company should be able to sustain its 12 to 15 percent growth rate of the past for a number of years to come.

Fort Howard Paper Company

	Net Sales (in millions)	Net Income (in millions)	Earnings per Share	Price Range*
1970	$80.4	$9.3	$1.41	NA
1966†	$51.6	$5.6	$0.84	NA
% Change	56	66	68	

* Since the original public offering, the shares have traded in a range between 39 and 27¾.
† 1965 statistics are not available.

General Reinsurance Corporation

Until recently the reinsurance industry has been one of the least-known growth areas in the United States.

What does a reinsurance company do, and what investment

advantages does it possess over standard insurance companies? A reinsurance company is simply an insurer of other insurance companies, mostly property and casualty companies. It takes risks off the hands of some twelve hundred property and casualty companies—either specified unusual risks or a broad range of risks described in a formal "treaty." Lloyd's of London is perhaps the best-known company in this field. General Reinsurance Corporation, an American company, is the most spectacularly successful.

Among the advantages that the reinsurance companies enjoy over primary insurers are: (1) they do not have any rate regulations; (2) business is written for special purposes; and (3) there is a low labor content. General Reinsurance, with 500 employees, wrote an estimated $270 million of business in 1971, and American Re-Insurance, a smaller but effective competitor, with 300 employees, will write about $200 million. A property or casualty company, on the other hand, would employ 3,000 to 4,000 people to handle the same amount of business.

Although numerous U.S. companies participate in the reinsurance market, and several foreign companies have played historic roles in reinsurance, three American companies have increasingly dominated the market. As already mentioned, General Reinsurance has been the most successful American reinsurer for many years, but in recent years American Re-Insurance and Employers Reinsurance Corporation (ERC) have also demonstrated consistent success. To be successful a reinsurance company must consistently improve underwriting profits and investment income. *General Reinsurance has reported underwriting profits for twenty-three consecutive years:* it has increased investment income twenty-two years in a row; and its net income after taxes for the last nine years.

The table on the following page shows the recent earnings record of the three principal American reinsurers.

Periodically, primary insurers and smaller reinsurers study (enviously) the profitable underwriting records of the major reinsurance companies and try their hands at the business. This

Per Share Earnings Record, Three Principal Reinsurance Companies

	General Reinsurance		ERC		American Re-Insurance	
	Net Investment Income After Taxes	Total Adjust. Earn.	Net Investment Income After Taxes	Total Adjust. Earn.	Net Investment Income Before Taxes	Total Adjust. Earn.
1970	$6.66	$7.70	$2.67	$3.54	$4.51	$4.58
1969	5.04	5.80	2.24	2.56	3.59	3.91
1968	4.16	4.78	2.36	2.43	3.09	2.69
1967	3.70	3.96	2.14	2.26	2.71	2.75
1966	3.17	3.79	1.96	1.96	2.53	1.01
1965	2.64	3.06	1.73	1.87	2.31	0.28

typically, and for several reasons, leads to a slowdown in the new business written by the major companies. However, the experience and skills of the specialist companies have withstood these periodic tests, and over the years the leaders have strengthened their position. The reinsurance market should continue to broaden in the years ahead, along with the growth of the overall fire and casualty market. Increases in insurable values, growing recognition of the need for insurance, development of new types of insurance to meet changing conditions, and emphasis on higher limits of insurance coverage are the factors expected to help. The principal reinsurers should continue to increase their market share in the United States and to improve their position in foreign markets.

General Reinsurance is not a brilliant innovator in the same sense as a number of other companies we discuss. Its success appears to depend more on experience in a highly specialized service business, a growing market and a powerful reputation in it, and strong financial management.

International Business Machines Corporation

No discussion of growth stocks would be complete without a serious review of IBM, the world's largest manufacturer of data-processing equipment and the sixth largest company in the world.* With a total market valuation that has ranged from $32 to $41 billion during the past twelve months, dollar holdings of IBM stock constitute more than 5 percent of all listed values on the New York Stock Exchange. An original investor who purchased and held 100 shares (plus all subsequent stock distributions) of Thomas J. Watson, Sr.'s Computer-Tabulating-Recording Company in 1914 for $2,750 would now be worth $21 million. At the 1971 annual meeting of IBM, one shareholder stood and pronounced, "If I found it necessary to raise some money, I would liquidate a painting or a jewel rather than sell a share of IBM."

* Ranked by sales.

International Business Machines Corporation

	Total Revenues (in millions)	Net Income (in millions)	Earnings per Share	Price Range
1970	$7,504	$1,018	$8.92	387–219
1965	$3,573	$ 477	$4.40	179–131
% Change	110	113	103	95

The time may have to come to question such shibboleths. The past five years have been a watershed in the history of the electronic data-processing industry and of IBM. For the first time students of the industry have begun questioning future growth and have inquired if IBM is a tree that can continue to grow to the sky.

Let us list a few of the factors shaping the outlook for the industry and the company.

1. Growth of markets outside the United States accelerated rapidly in the 1960s and became the dominant source of data-processing market expansion. In 1970 IBM's earnings from operations outside the United States exceeded 50 percent of consolidated earnings. In 1970 *domestic earnings declined.*

2. The appearance of computer-leasing companies on a large scale between 1966 and 1968 led to a burst of outright computer sales by IBM in relation to rentals, and this development disturbed IBM's historically stable lease-earnings growth.*

3. Heightened competition from peripheral equipment companies and the background presence of the U.S. Department of Justice have forced IBM to "unbundle" its hardware and its software. The IBM customer is now able to separate the cost of services from the cost of the apparatus, to evaluate the different elements, and to use alternate programming and peripheral products if he so wishes.

---

* IBM sold computers to the leasing companies, who, in turn, leased them to users. The leasing companies were, in essence, finance companies willing to assume the risk that the computers would not become obsolete before they were fully depreciated.

4. Unchivalric but competent peripheral equipment manufacturers have forced price competition upon IBM.

5. The curtailment of U.S. government expenditures for defense and aerospace programs, coinciding with rising cost pressures and a recession in the U.S. economy in 1969 and 1970, forced the first meaningful contraction in overall computer utilization in this country. When faced with reduced revenues and shrinking margins, many companies, both in government-related activities and in civilian manufacturing, found themselves overcomputerized and revised their data-processing requirements downward. IBM experienced its first significant lapses in computer rental renewals. At the end of a rental period (thirty days), the IBM lessee would simply discontinue his rental for some of his equipment and return it to IBM. To preserve margins, IBM has restricted salary increases and made selected personnel reductions.

6. Faced with intensive, prolonged R&D requirements, extraordinary capital needs, and deteriorating prospects for an attractive return on their investments, two primary electronic data-processing manufacturers have given up the ghost. General Electric has sold its worldwide computer operations to Honeywell. RCA has announced that it will close down all of its computer activities and will sell its U.S. and Canadian customer base to Sperry Rand. It has taken a huge nonrecurring write-off. Will the consolidation of the industry into fewer but stronger hands tend to help or hurt IBM, which still holds the lion's share of the market?

7. For the first time in its corporate history IBM is operating without a member of the Watson family at the helm. The impact of the family on the standards of this company has been profound. Both Thomas J. Watson, Jr. and his brother Arthur have retired from active management responsibilities, one for reasons of health, the other to pursue interests in the diplomatic world. Direction has been turned over to T. Vincent Learson and a team of his selection. What the intangible and tangible consequences of this transfer of corporate responsibility will be, no one can predict.

IBM moves into the 1970s with a new computer series, the 370 group. Like its predecessors, the 370 series is designed to upgrade and replace computers in the field—in this case 35,000 IBM 360s —and to build new markets. The 370 is several times more power-ful than its predecessor, and sells for about 25 percent more. The company also has new copying devices and a variety of other new products, but in view of its enormous size, entries into new fields cannot have much impact on overall results.

During the decade ahead we believe that the domestic data-processing industry will continue to grow at a faster rate than the economy, but that this rate may be around 10 percent rather than the 15 to 20 percent figure of the past decade. IBM's managerial, technical, and marketing competence is such that we see no reason why it cannot continue to keep pace with the industry and thus retain its market share. (Keep in mind it spends more than $500 million annually on research, more than the gross data-processing revenues of several competitors!) Given continued good overseas growth—superimposed on the domestic growth rates—IBM may be able to increase its earnings on a worldwide basis at a rate of about 12 percent a year for most of this decade. Is this enough to make it an interesting investment at the kind of price-earnings ratios it has sold at in the last decade?

It may well be that because of its enormous size, the gradual conversion of its computers into commodities, and the inevitable slowing of the growth of its markets, IBM will look more like General Motors at the end of the decade than the IBM to which we have become accustomed. Like General Motors a decade ago, we believe it is moving from growth to maturity. . . .

Johnson & Johnson

In a quiet manner Johnson & Johnson has had one of the most extraordinarily successful records of the past decade, arriving at the billion-dollar annual sales level in 1970. About 80 percent of the company's volume now comes from a broad range of surgical, pharmaceutical, and hygienic products, including surgical dressings, contraceptives, and baby-care products. One of the best-known Johnson & Johnson products is Band-Aids.

Johnson & Johnson

	Sales (in millions)	Net Income (in millions)	Earnings per Share	Price Range
1970	$1,002	$84	$1.51	60–37
1965	$ 576	$34	$0.64	20–12
% Change	74	147	136	203

There appears to be no reason why the company should not keep moving forward in the years ahead. In 1970 alone Johnson & Johnson increased its worldwide sales by $100 million. Many fine companies, including several discussed in this section, work for a generation to achieve total annual sales of that magnitude.

The management of Johnson & Johnson is famous for its in-accessibility to security analysts. It relies on its record to demonstrate its success.

In a rare moment of self-appraisal, management once described the company's progress as "both dynamic and orderly." By steadily broadening its product line and by expanding its penetration of worldwide markets, the company has built momentum and stability, increasing its immunity to the ups-and-downs of a given product cycle or local economic disturbance.

There is no part of the world that does not need (and virtually none that does not use) the health services provided by Johnson & Johnson. While the company has been long established in overseas markets, in 1970 it established new subsidiaries in Nigeria, Kenya, and Thailand. It now operates companies in 33 countries outside the United States, and has nearly 33,000 licensed trademarks in more than 100 countries.

As with so many multinational corporations, Johnson & Johnson has lately grown more rapidly outside the United States than within.

In 1970 international results comprised 30 percent of consolidated sales and 33 percent of pretax earnings. Overseas earnings of $30 million exceeded total earnings six years earlier.

Johnson & Johnson has been willing both to acquire companies that broaden its markets and to dispose of those that do not fit. Over the years, the establishment or the acquisition of Ortho Pharmaceuticals (1940), Ethicon (1949), McNeil Laboratories (1959), Jelco (1964), and Pitman-Moore (1969) have helped expedite the company's development of ethical* pharmaceuticals, its hospital supply business, and its move into veterinary products.

The fruits of the company's research include many ethical drugs, new types of disposable products for use in operating and delivery rooms, and a variety of new products for the dental market. Research is decentralized, along with conduct of business as a whole. Overall, more than 1,000 scientists work in 45 laboratories throughout the world.

Johnson & Johnson combines broad technical skill with superb worldwide marketing. Its research effort is far broader and deeper, say, than that of a company like Avon. Its marketing approach is more orthodox. The combination of the two, coupled with superb financial condition, promises *consistent* above-average earnings growth—we believe 15 percent per year—for years to come.

S. S. Kresge Company

Kresge is that rare animal: a large organization that recognized the maturity of its basic business and moved dramatically down a new path. Since 1962 Kresge has emerged as the fastest-growing large retail organization in the United States. Its K-Mart stores have outdistanced all other discounters. Kresge has opened more than four hundred such stores, principally in the Southern and

---

* Ethical drugs require a doctor's prescription; proprietary drugs (like aspirin) do not.

Western regions of the United States, while closing many of its unprofitable variety units. *Its sales have increased from $450 million in 1962 to more than $2.5 billion in less than a decade,* a growth in some ways more dramatic than Xerox's.

S. S. Kresge Company

	Sales (in millions)	Net Income (in millions)	Earnings per Share	Price Range	No. of Stores	Net Profit per Store
1970	$2,559	$67	$1.85	69–33	1,073	$62,000
1965	$ 851	$22	$0.66	14–8	895	$23,000
% Change	201	205	180	364	20	170

In an industry that is notorious for the poor quality of its lower-echelon personnel, Kresge has placed strong emphasis on the development of a large pool of experienced and motivated store managers to sustain its store expansion program and to support the progress of existing stores. Kresge's management training program now has more than two thousand men. By the time he reaches his career destination, a K-Mart store manager will have been given two tours of duty as manager of a variety or Jupiter store, and time in grade as an assistant store manager for K-Mart. K-Mart management has grown from within, in contrast to most other retail operations which find their management from external sources. Most K-Mart managers earn more than $30,000 per annum, substantially more than the $15,000 to $20,000 paid to store managers by competitors. The consequence of this is that fewer than 1 percent of K-Mart store managers left the company during 1969.

When K-Mart moves into a new geographic area, it attempts to secure a large segment of the retail discount business done in that community. In 1969, for example, seven K-Mart stores accounted for almost 30 percent of the volume done by all discount outlets in the greater Atlanta metropolitan area. This concentration gives K-Mart the advertising muscle that so many smaller retailers lack. In Atlanta Kresge flooded the market with more than 2.5 times as much advertising lineage as all its competitors but still kept advertising as a small percent of its sales dollar.

K-Marts, which now account for more than 80 percent of Kresge's total sales and earnings, will be opened at the rate of seventy-five stores per year for the next four or five years. Combined with continued profit margin improvement, which generally takes place each year for several years after new stores are opened, the new store expansion program should permit Kresge to continue its remarkable unbroken earnings growth at a 15 to 20 percent pace for the foreseeable future.

Lubrizol Corporation

The story of Lubrizol, like that of so many American success stories, begins with the automobile industry. In Cleveland in 1928, several brothers named Smith responded to the needs of the fledgling automobile industry for special-purpose lubricant compounds. Since then the company has steadily expanded its expertise in the specialty chemical business until it has become the dominant worldwide supplier of chemical additives for use in lubricants for automobiles, buses, trucks, and off-the-road equipment; for use in industrial and marine lubricants; and for gasoline and fuel oil. It also supplies chemicals for use in metal finishing and in plastic formulations.

The Chemical Fund, in its third-quarter 1971 report, describes organizations like Lubrizol as "research-oriented companies which produce specialty products and are *thus able to concentrate their sales generally not subject to the heavy competition and narrow profit margins of commodity-oriented companies.*" (Emphasis ours.)

In its 1970 annual report Lubrizol makes reference to the criteria which have produced consistent progress:

A strong commitment to research . . .

A marketing philosophy which places the highest emphasis on customer service.

An active capital improvement program to upgrade manufacturing plants and provide lower cost operations with adequate reserve capacity.

A dedication to noteworthy employees through recognition of individual dignity and rewards based on individual achievement.

These words help explain how this company tripled its sales and quintupled its earnings from 1960 to 1970. They explain why it earns 11.7 percent after taxes on sales and 18 percent on shareholders' equity.

By spending more than 7 percent of sales on research, by focusing on specialty markets, by providing special customer services, Lubrizol has grown consistently, has earned a high return on invested capital and maintained a superb balance sheet. The company has never made an acquisition.

Its products rarely receive public attention (in fact they are anonymous), and so the company's achievements have not received the same wide acknowledgment as, say, Xerox, Johnson & Johnson, or Avon Products.

Lubrizol Corporation

	Sales (in millions)	Net Income (in millions)	Earnings per Share	Price Range
1970	$187	$22	$1.08	39–20
1965	$ 93	$10	$0.50	8–5
% Change	101	120	116	354

The important factors of safety and environmental protection are forcing the auto industry to tighten and change many specifications. Often these changes create demands for new and more sophisticated lubricants. As vehicles converted from standard shifts to automatic transmissions (as they have largely done here and are doing overseas), and as rear-axle posi-traction devices are adopted, the requirements for additives in lubricants expand. In 1970 more than 45 percent of the company's sales were derived from additive formulations containing one or more chemical ingredients developed during the last five years. Of the company's 2,900 employees, more than 700 are engaged in research and testing. The company has never experienced a strike or unit stoppage, and none of its U.S. employees belong to a union.

If we measure this company against the standards we have earlier defined in our search for successful companies, it meets them all. It is no longer an undiscovered company, as it was five years ago—merely a unique one.

McDonald's Corporation

How often have you been on the highway and been asked "Where can we eat?" by your children? McDonald's has provided the answer. It is a company that has responded to a modern need —for "fast food service." It is the only company among many food franchise service operations that emerged unscathed from the difficult economic environment of 1969–1971. It has made it possible for millions of Americans to eat and run, and it is carrying this habit overseas.

What has been demonstrated is that this business is not as simple as it earlier appeared. In the last two years, with the exception of McDonald's, almost all fast-food franchise companies have experienced trouble of some kind, which has been reflected in earnings difficulties, slowdowns in expansions, and stock price collapse. McDonald's staying power can be attributed to its management's boldness in applying capital to the development of a powerful national distribution system and, through a major advertising commitment, to the development of a proprietary product image. The company's financial controls are sophisticated. It manages its underlying real estate business in a professional way. And, not least, it sells tasty food.

When you eat at McDonald's, your choice is limited to hamburgers, cheeseburgers, fish sandwiches, french-fried potatoes, milk shakes, milk, coffee, hot chocolate, and certain soft drinks. Before new products are added to the menu, they are carefully analyzed to determine their incremental sales value and their potential impact on existing products. McDonald's is now testing the addition of chicken to its menus. Because of the sizable investment that must be made to serve chicken (much more than was involved in the development of the "Big Mac"), it will be test-marketed with care.

The keys to McDonald's future growth lie in its ability to impose additional sales volume on outstanding units, and to add profitable units to the chain.

McDonald's Corporation

	Sales (in millions)	Net Income (in millions)	Earnings per Share	Price Range	Stores Company-Operated	Franchised
1970	$193	$18	$0.99	31–18	384	1,208
1965	$ 43	$ 4	$0.25	5–2	143	595
% Change	349	350	296	600	169	103

McDonald's national advertising not only strengthens its proprietary image (much of the advertising is aimed at your children, who are very influential in telling you where to stop when you are out for a drive), but also assists the company's expansion program. Most of McDonald's expansion comes in areas that have already been exposed to such advertising. The company's message has already reached your children by the time the unit is open for business. With name and reputation established, volume builds quickly, and with it comes prompt profitability. Finally, McDonald's national prominence has made it expensive for regional fast-food chains to compete in new areas.

McDonald's has utilized price increases carefully to offset rising costs, and to protect profit margins, but not as the basis for margin improvement.

McDonald's has met a specific need of the driving public—a need that exists all over our world—for good food, served speedily and economically. It is now taking this service concept outside the continental United States (just as Avon has taken its unique distribution techniques), and it will be fascinating to observe the response.

Minnesota Mining & Manufacturing Company

3M started the second half of the sixties with sales of $1 billion, about what Johnson & Johnson has today. Continued new product development, growing worldwide markets, and attention to costs have paid off for 3M in results that, while never spectacular, were far better than average.

Minnesota Mining & Manufacturing Company

	Sales (in millions)	Net Income (in millions)	Earnings per Share	Market Value per Share	No. of Employees (in thousands)
1970*	$1,687.3	$187.7	$3.35	115–71	65.8
1965*	$1,000.3	$116.4	$2.18	71–54	49.0
% Change	68.7	61.2	53.6	48.8	34.2

* Fiscal period ended December 31.

Faced with the constant pressure of rising wage costs, 3M has achieved much of its earnings improvement by increased employee productivity. During these years, sales rose from $20,400 per annum per employee to $25,600 per employee. While a part of this improvement reflects price inflation, the bulk represents genuine operating efficiencies.

3M products reach into every aspect of everyday life. More than 4,000 people serve in research and product development, creating the more than 35,000 products sold throughout the world. From its original work in the field of abrasives and coatings have come products that serve almost every market one can think of: "Stop" signs that we pass on the highways, traffic control systems, new artificial Tartan turf, photographic products, tapes that will be used by Sony in their video cassettes, pharmaceutical products produced by newly acquired companies. 3M has used acquisitions effectively to broaden existing lines and services without distorting its balance sheet, or in any way destroying its orderly expansion patterns.

As a consequence of remaining true to its basic objectives, and of building a management in depth to accompany its growth, 3M today is a major company that should continue to grow at 8 to 10 percent annually for many years.

The Perkin-Elmer Corporation

Perkin-Elmer describes its business succinctly in its 1971 annual report:

Perkin-Elmer's basic business is scientific instrumentation. Its markets include almost every industry, medical research institutions, hospital and police laboratories, colleges and universities, and government agencies involved in advanced scientific systems.

Perkin-Elmer laboratory analytical instruments measure and analyze practically every facet of man's material life—his food, his water, his blood, his fabrics, his medicines, his machines, the air he breathes. These instruments range in price from a few hundred dollars to more than $50,000.

Precise optics and electro-optical systems developed by the company are employed in space and national security applications such as astronomy and space science, reconnaissance, missile tracking and re-entry studies, earth resources research, atmosphere analysis and night vision.

Other Perkin-Elmer products include high vacuum equipment, electronic components, laser metrology equipment, and instruments for aircraft and missile flight control and guidance.

These products are marketed throughout the world; Perkin-Elmer derives approximately one-third of its sales from overseas markets. It also benefits from the new product development resources of long-established manufacturing subsidiaries in West Germany and the United Kingdom and an affiliation in Japan.

Despite its dependence on defense spending, Perkin-Elmer has increased earnings for fifteen consecutive years. It has a brilliant management headed by Chester W. Nimitz, Jr., chairman of the board and president. Never has managerial excellence been more in evidence than in fiscal 1971. That year the company increased its net income 11 percent in the face of a $32 million, or 16 percent, revenue reduction.

A number of investors will undoubtedly worry about the continuing importance of U.S. government business to Perkin-Elmer. It still accounted for 47 percent of revenues in the fiscal year ended July 31, 1971.

We do not wish to minimize this problem but would point out that: (1) profit margins in commercial business are higher than in government business, so the contribution of the latter to total earnings is smaller than the above percentage suggests; (2) much of Perkin-Elmer's government business is research oriented and thus is not as sensitive to swings in spending for large weapons systems as other defense-oriented concerns; and (3) cutbacks in government defense and research spending may have run their course.

It has become fashionable in investment circles to stress the attractiveness of consumer-goods companies and to disparage "high-technology" concerns, which, almost by definition, do a good deal of business with the federal government.

Among the technology companies, Perkin-Elmer appears to offer a number of important and unusual features:

- A genuinely strong area of technological specialization (optics).
- A technology that has broad commercial as well as defense application.
- An unusually large overseas business.

- A management that has demonstrated it can effectively roll with the punches when it comes to coping with the uncertainties of defense spending.
- A strong balance sheet.

Perhaps technology companies no longer meet your fancy. But if you find one you like, compare it with this to see if it's really more interesting.

The Perkin-Elmer Corporation

	Revenues (in millions)	Net Income (in millions)	Earnings per Share	Price Range
F 1971*	$171.4	$9.0	$1.36	55–29
F 1966*	$ 88.4	$4.4	$0.71	20–12
% Change	94	105	92	163

* Fiscal period ended July 31.

Pinkerton's Inc.

When we think of a private eye, a "Pinkerton man" automatically comes to mind. In fact, the term "private eye" comes from an early Pinkerton trademark, an eye with the inscription, "We never sleep."

Pinkerton's history as a service company providing investigative services dates back to 1850. Pinkerton's organized the first secret service to obtain military intelligence for the Union Army, and it arranged for the protection of Abraham Lincoln on his first trip from Springfield, Illinois, to Washington for his inauguration (it didn't do so well later on). Until the recent passing of Robert A. Pinkerton, a great-grandson of the founder, a member of the family had continuously been at the helm. A critical element in Pinkerton's leadership in the field of protective services has been its name and reputation.

Pinkerton's is the quintessential service company. It provides specialized services in a particular field more efficiently and economically than customers—corporations, hospitals, universities, and sometimes even governments—can organize and support themselves.

Pinkerton's is the largest company providing security and protective services in the United States and Canada. The company furnishes uniformed guards and other personnel to handle plant protection, traffic control (especially at airports and sporting events), and security checks on a full-time, intermittent, or temporary basis. Assistance is provided in making surveys and in developing protective plans. The installation and servicing of protective devices round out the company's programs.

Although the business is dependent on labor (some thirty thousand employees), inflationary pressures have not been a particular problem. Cost increases have been passed on to the customer. (Service companies, unlike most manufacturing concerns, run no risk of import competition as they raise prices.) The relation of revenues to labor costs has remained constant, and union problems are virtually nonexistent.

Overall market penetration by protective services appears to be approximately 35 percent—that is, nearly two-thirds of potential customers still provide their own guard service. The company's objective is to increase "revenues from Security Services by more than $1 million per month over the same month the preceding year. At the end of 1970, we had achieved an unbroken record of 35 consecutive months of such increases," according to the 1970 annual report.

Pinkerton's has surpassed the sales and earnings achievements of all its competitors in the protective services field. Consequently its earnings record has not gone unrecognized by the stock market. Its 40+ price-earnings ratio in relation to 1970 earnings of $1.76 per share represents a premium multiple even in relation to other high-grade growth companies.

Unfortunately, crime is here to stay. We believe the demand for Pinkerton's services will continue to grow handsomely for a long time to come, with increased penetration of the market more than offsetting the impact of occasional business recessions.

At the close of 1970 Pinkerton's cash and marketable securities of $8.9 million exceeded total current liabilities of $8.4 million. The company has no debt.

Pinkerton's Inc.

	Revenues (in millions)	Net Income (in millions)	Earnings per Share	Price Range
1970	$135	$4.9	$1.76	83–44
1965	$ 67	$1.6	$0.57	NA
% Change	102	206	209	

The Stanley Works

Not spectacular in its public relations, not promotion oriented, and without the drumbeating support of any investment banking firm, this company has increased its sales 150 percent during the last decade, its net income 200 percent, and its earnings per share 111 percent. Its return on invested capital in 1970 amounted to 15.8 percent.

The Stanley Works

	Sales (in millions)	Net Income (in millions)	Earnings per Share	Price Range
1970	$257.6	$12.5	$1.75	25–19
1965*	$198.3	$ 9.7	$1.34†	15–12
% Change	30	29	30	63

* 1965 restated to give effect to the pooling of interests resulting from the merger with Amerock on August 1, 1966.
† Earnings before Extraordinary Items.

We cannot pretend that the Stanley Works is a "true" growth company that keeps creating new markets for itself through innovational genius. It has few products or services that are unique. It just keeps moving steadily ahead in a variety of commercial, residential, and consumer building markets. More than 100,000 Stanley hinges will open and close doors in the World Trade

Center in New York City. A Stanley air curtain is used at the main entrance to the Metropolitan Museum of Art in the same city. You use Stanley products every day. They include the hardware on your kitchen cabinets or your garage door, or the tools in your workshop.

Management has been the key. Careful planning has enabled it to cope with swings in the building markets the company serves; to make acquisitions that helped, in a modest way, to reinforce growth; and to make divestitures of divisions that were not meeting stringent corporate financial standards. Perhaps most significantly, management has greatly improved employee productivity, as illustrated by the table below:

The Stanley Works

	Sales per Employee	Net Before Taxes per Employee	Earnings Before Taxes as % of Sales
1970	$19,148	$1,768	9.2
1961	$13,185	$1,065	8.1
% Change	45.0	66.0	14.0

This isn't as glamorously successful a company as a number of others we have discussed, but we like its careful, no-nonsense New England virtues. Characteristically, it has paid dividends in every year since 1877.

Tampax Incorporated

Starting with a $300,000 capital investment in 1936, Tampax is the exception that proves the rule, a *one-product company* that nothing seems to stop. The company has been manufacturing tampons for feminine use for thirty-five years—and thirty-five years after it entered business it is still manufacturing only tampons. Sales have risen in each and every year, pretax net income has risen in parallel. Only the excess-profit-tax years of World War II and the Korean War prevented the company from recording similar uninterrupted growth in net income.

Tampax Incorporated

	Sales (in millions)	Net Income (in millions)	Earnings per Share	Price Range
1970	$76.5	$18.6	$6.58	229–147
1965	$41.9	$ 9.6	$3.39	130–94
% Change	83	94	94	68

Founding management still sits in the executive chair. The company has no funded debt, no preferred stock, and its cash and equivalent assets exceed its current liabilities several fold.

The corporation's pretax margins approach 50 percent and still the management remains ultra-cost-conscious. Its manufacturing facilities and costs are constantly improved; there is a kind of intensity to detail here that flows from having only one product to worry about. (Several years ago, when Manhattan rents became too stiff, the company moved its headquarters to suburban Long Island.)

In recent years Tampax has experienced dedicated competition from several major challengers who have long been producers of other types of catamenial products (over the years it has competed against at least one hundred competitive tampon products). Yet it retains market dominance with close to 75 percent of the domestic tampon market.

During recent years the tampon segment of the domestic catamenial market has shown acceleration from its 12 percent compounded rate of the 1959–1969 decade. To illustrate better the domestic market for catamenial products, we present below the salient figures:

Market Growth Relative to Tampax Revenue Growth *Catamenial Products*

Year	Total (in millions)	Sanitary Napkins (in millions)	Tampons (in millions)	Tampons as % of Total	Tampax Revenues (in millions)
1970	$283.2	$185.3	$97.9	35	$76.5
1969	266.9	180.5	86.4	32	68.1
1964	214.2	169.3	44.9	21	38.0
1959	178.4	150.7	27.7	16	NA
1954	154.2	133.9	20.3	13	NA

Source: Drug Trade News.

Tampax's total worldwide sales volume has yet to reach the $100 million level; it will surpass that figure in 1972. Of its total business approximately 25 percent comes from abroad.

Can growth last? That question has been raised perennially by cynics who doubt the viability of one-product companies. In recent years concern over a better product has been a smaller question mark. The specter most constantly raised has been the possible advent and use by powerful competitors of national TV advertising. While this idea has been tried locally during late-night movies in independent stations and also overseas, it has not yet received approval of the National Association of Broadcasters Television Code Board. And what if it did come about—as we suspect it will? Tampax, with the best-known and most accepted name in the business, is likely to be a beneficiary, not a victim. If we consider Tampax's product not simply as a product alone but as a product *and* its brand name, the company appears to have built an extraordinarily strong position.

Xerox Corporation

The following table tells part of the Xerox story for the last five years:

Xerox Corporation

	Total Operat- ing Reve- nues (in millions)	Rentals, Service, and Royalties (in millions)	Re- search and Develop- ment (in millions)	Net Income (in millions)	Earnings per Share	Price Range
1970	$1,718.6	$1,343.3	$97.5	$187.7	$2.40	116–65
1965	$ 548.8	$ 327.8	$38.2	$ 65.7	$0.92	72–32
% Change	213	310	155	186	161	74

The part of the story that does not show is the extent to which the company would have improved upon this outstanding performance if it had not been bitten by the acquisition bug.

Xerox has built a strong proprietary position in a powerful new market—copying and short-run duplicating. Like the truly great growth companies, it has created these markets with new products and services that did not heretofore exist. Its underlying business has been strong enough to hide mistakes in evaluating and acquiring a number of concerns in the fields of education and data-processing. The biggest mistake appears to have been the 1969 acquisition of Scientific Data Systems, a computer company, for 10 million Xerox common shares (then worth approximately $1 billion). Shortly thereafter, the computer industry began to suffer from the economic slowdown and retrenchment of government spending for defense and aerospace activities. Xerox's Data Systems Division, of which SDS was the major component, experienced a drop in revenues from $125 million in 1969 to $83 million in 1970. Pretax earnings of $24 million in 1969 were transformed into a $36 million pretax loss in 1970 (including inventory writedowns). It is a tribute to the company's overall strength that it could take this loss in stride. And it may be that Xerox has the time and the muscle to turn its computer and educational companies around so that by the end of this decade it will be stronger, not weaker, as a result of the acquisitions in question. But meanwhile they are a drag.

One wonders why Xerox moved into these new fields. Did it take a hard enough look at the underlying fundamentals? Or was it caught up in overly optimistic Wall Street appraisals? Did it suffer from an IBM syndrome? IBM had made an earlier acquisition in the educational field, and it announced subsequently that it would invade Xerox's copying market. Xerox followed with its own entry into education, and then invaded IBM's "turf" with its SDS merger. Or did Xerox have a secret concern about the long-range growth potential of the copying and duplicating business? Where is Xerox headed from here?

The paperwork revolution is far from over. In many countries it is gathering momentum, and Xerox, like many of the other companies we have discussed, has a powerful overseas position. We have confidence in the company's ability to retain a strong position in its major markets, and we continue to have confidence that its markets will grow. The new 4000 family copying device is the latest in a long series of powerful product innovations. The 4000 machine is the first that can automatically copy on both sides of the paper, thus cutting paper costs in half. The company continues to build a strong sales and service organization, and, as indicated in the earlier table, has almost tripled its research and development outlays in the last five years.

On the other hand, it is difficult to foresee Xerox achieving the 213 percent revenue increase and 186 percent net income rise of the last five years. *Market growth must slow somewhat.* Furthermore, we believe growth will be more sensitive to general business conditions.

In our judgment a growth rate of 12 to 15 percent per annum for earnings per share is a more likely prospect than the flamboyant rates of the past. This is still mighty good, and with appropriate timing investors are still likely to make an adequate return in these shares over the next decade.

We said at the beginning of this chapter that this group of sixteen companies were being presented as paradigms of corporate success, not as specific stock purchase recommendations (in determining, for yourself, whether these or other individual growth stocks are attractive purchases, we recommend careful consideration of the next chapter, "A Note on Timing").

What models have emerged?

Stanley Works seems to us an example of the corporate plugger. Success here depends on managerial tenacity and control. The company is not a brilliant innovator, although it does sell a broad range of superior products. (Illinois Tool Works is another fine company of this sort.)

Tampax is a one-product company (here we could have used Dr. Pepper). Success depends critically on building market share and defending the product from competitive inroads by creating a powerful brand name.

Fort Howard, Lubrizol, and *Perkin-Elmer* rely primarily on specialized technologies that serve niches in broad industrial markets. These companies do a solid marketing job, too, but it is less important than in the case of others. *DEKALB* is comparable to these three companies except that it operates in agriculture instead of industry. Its research cycle is long—like Polaroid's— and the chances for a large speculative success (the development of hybrid wheat, for example) are better than in the case of the other three.

General Reinsurance and *Pinkerton's* are service companies par excellence. Specialization and experience are the keys to their success.

Kresge and *McDonald's* represent another kind of success story. They are both retailers; they are both developing national brand-name acceptance for their outlets. They depend importantly, for growth, on the combination of adding new outlets and improving the profitability of *all* outlets.

Avon is another model: an all-powerful, unique marketing system.

Johnson & Johnson and *3M* have harnessed strong (but not unique) marketing systems to impressive research and engineering abilities. Both companies sell many low-priced items, and many of these are disposable (think of the striking commercial similarity between Band-Aids and Scotch tape). Eastman Kodak and Procter & Gamble are companies of the same sort. Sears today seems more closely related to this kind of enterprise than it does to Kresge, since it depends more on developing strong brand attachment to individual products and services than it does to expanding the number of individual retail outlets.

IBM and *Xerox* are like Johnson & Johnson and 3M, except that they market more complex, expensive equipment that is, to an important degree, leased.

Disney, oddly enough, reminds us of Polaroid. It has depended since its inception on the genius of one man. Each company is, in its field, unique. The cycle of new product development is long. As one looks ahead to the next hoped-for round of earnings expansion, there is always a great deal of uncertainty. They are both fascinating companies. Both are still quite small in terms of revenues, but their market equities (the total market value of all outstanding shares) are huge.

One is impressed with the important role that marketing has played in the success of these companies—not only the introduction of a steady stream of new products, but the building of sales forces, sales managers, incentive plans, advertising budgets, and the formulation of strategic pricing decisions. What kind of a stock would Xerox have been during the last ten years if it had decided to sell its copying machines—as Addressograph sells addressing equipment—instead of leasing them and *charging for each copy made?*

One is impressed, too, with the ability of most of these companies to move rapidly and effectively overseas.

George Odiorne, the brilliant dean of the Graduate School of Business Administration at the University of Utah, stresses the importance of *control* as well as innovation in a corporation's destiny. Without financial (and other) discipline, innovation takes place on quicksand. With control, innovation provides orderly, sustained growth. Certainly the companies we have described in this chapter appear to be able to put that rare and wonderful combination of discipline and creativity together—in varying combinations, with different emphasis, but with phenomenal collective success.

9

A Note on Timing

Before concluding this discussion of stock selection with a chapter on investing in problem companies, we'd like to take a moment to help you with the second of the two major difficulties involved in building your portfolio of successful, or growth, companies. The first difficulty, covered in Chapter 5, concerned the determination of the potential market size for the products of truly innovative companies. (For example, how large will consumer demand be for the entertainment provided by Walt Disney World? And if the Florida installation succeeds, how many more can be built?) The second difficulty, which we come to now, is the problem of the price you should pay for the shares of a company you are convinced will become or will continue to be successful in the terms we have established.

This is a problem of *timing*. You have made a decision that you want a piece of a particular corporate action. The question is not *whether* to buy the stock but *when*.

Many of the companies we have described in the previous chapter as successful are selling at premium price-earnings ratios, as indicated in the table opposite:

	Current Price 12/31/71	Earnings per Share Estimates*		P-E Ratio	
		1971	1972	1971	1972
Avon Products	106	$1.90	$2.20	55.8X	48.2X
DEKALB AgResearch†	48	1.87A	2.30	25.7	20.9
Walt Disney	133	2.00	2.50	66.5	53.2
Fort Howard Paper	37	1.70	1.90	21.8	19.5
General Reinsurance	310	10.00	12.00	31.0	25.8
IBM	346	9.25	10.25	37.4	33.8
Johnson & Johnson	98	1.85	2.20	53.0	44.5
Kresge	101	2.50	3.20	40.4	31.6
Lubrizol	55	1.20	1.35–1.40	45.8	40.7–39.3
McDonald's	77	1.30	1.70	59.2	45.3
3M	134	3.75	4.20	35.7	31.9
Perkin-Elmer‡	58	1.36A	1.45	42.6	40.0
Pinkerton's	73	2.00	2.35	36.5	31.1
Stanley Works	33	2.05	2.30	16.1	14.3
Tampax	328	7.80	8.80	42.1	37.3
Xerox	126	2.70	3.10–3.15	46.7	40.6–40.0

A = Actual.
* All estimates made by authors in December, 1971.
† Fiscal year ended August 31.
‡ Fiscal year ended July 30.

These stocks *should* sell at premiums, otherwise why be successful? The question is how high a price should you pay at a given moment, or over a period of time, in order to earn the 10 to 12 percent annual return you are looking for.

To determine this you must engage in a dialogue with your adviser in which you make the best possible estimate of the earnings growth rate and dividend payments for the company in which you contemplate the investment. We present in the table on the next page, our estimated earnings growth rates for the sixteen companies we have been discussing and their current dividends.

In forecasting growth rates, you and your adviser should try to look ahead three years. One year is not enough, and five is too long. Then, together, you must make a judgment on whether the price-earnings ratio for a given company three years hence will be higher or lower than it is now. If the company is at present rela-

	Est. Growth Rate 1972–1975	Current Dividend
Avon Products	12–13%	$1.30
DEKALB AgResearch	12	0.17
Walt Disney	15	0.20
Fort Howard Paper	12–15	0.50
General Reinsurance	15–20	0.60
IBM	12	5.20
Johnson & Johnson	15	0.40
Kresge	15–20	0.50
Lubrizol	12–13	0.40
McDonald's	20–25	–0–
3M	8–10	1.85
Perkin-Elmer	15	0.40
Pinkerton's	15	0.70
Stanley Works	10	0.80
Tampax	15	4.00
Xerox	12–15	0.80

tively undiscovered and selling at a modest price-earnings ratio and earnings materialize as you anticipate, then perhaps the multiple in three years will be higher. On the other hand, if the company is already large, is selling at a premium, and the only thing you can be sure of is that it will be growing at a somewhat slower rate three years from now, then assume a lower P-E ratio at that time. Once you've determined the growth rate and P-E ratio three years from now, turn to the next table.

Let's take a couple of examples to illustrate how the table works:

First, Avon. Its estimated per share earnings in 1971 were $1.90. The growth rate we expect for the next three years is 12 percent. Find 12 percent in the first column of the table. Look immediately to the right. The figure there is $1.40. This is what $1.00 of earnings will become if it grows at 12 percent compounded for 3 years. To find what earnings of $1.90—*Avon*'s earnings—will become if they grow at 12 percent annually, multiply $1.90 by $1.40. The figure is $2.66. Avon today sells at 100, or a multiple of roughly

Annual Growth Rate	What $1.00 of Earnings Will Become in 3 Years at Given Growth Rate	The Price-Earnings Ratio You Can Pay Today If You Want to Make a 10% Annual Capital Gain and You Expect the Price-Earnings Ratio in Three Years to Be	
		15X	30X
4%	$1.12	12.6	25.3
5	1.16	13.1	26.2
6	1.19	13.4	26.8
7	1.23	13.9	27.7
8	1.26	14.2	28.4
9	1.30	14.7	29.3
10	1.33	15.0	30.0
11	1.37	15.5	30.9
12	1.40	15.8	31.6
13	1.44	16.2	32.5
14	1.48	16.7	33.4
15	1.52	17.1	34.3
16	1.56	17.6	35.2
17	1.60	18.0	36.1
18	1.64	18.5	37.0
19	1.69	19.1	38.1
20	1.73	19.5	39.0
25	1.95	22.0	44.0
30	2.20	24.8	49.6
35	2.46	27.7	55.5
40	2.74	30.9	61.8
45	3.05	34.4	68.8
50	3.38	38.1	76.2

50 times 1971 earnings. It seems doubtful that this multiple will increase. Suppose it drops to 35 times in three years? Thirty-five times earnings of $2.66 in three years produces a stock price of 93, a little lower than the price today. Obviously, *on the basis of these assumptions,* the timing isn't very good.

Let's take Kresge. It, too, sells for 100. Earnings in 1971 are estimated at $2.50 per share, so it sells at 40 times earnings. We expect earnings to grow at 17 percent annually for the next three years. Using the table on page 123 in the same way as described above, we calculate that earnings will climb to $4.00 in 1974. Suppose Kresge's price-earnings ratio dropped to 35 at the end of the period? The stock would sell for 140 (35 × $4.00). What kind of a return is that? Divide 140 by the 100, the starting price, and you get 1.40. Look at column 2 for the number closest to 1.40, and then look to the left-hand column for the annual return—in this case about 12 percent. In other words, you meet your objectives, without allowing for the annual return you receive from dividends (in Kresge's case the dividend is 50 cents per share, and so increases the 12 percent return to 12.5 percent). In short, given these assumptions, the timing may be appropriate.

What of the two right-hand columns? These show what price-earnings ratio you can afford to pay today if you assume the stock you buy today will sell at 15 times earnings or at 30 times earnings three years from now and you want to earn a minimum return of 10 percent per annum, exclusive of dividends.

Let's assume you believe General Reinsurance will sell at 30 times earnings three years from now. You have estimated its growth rate at 15 percent. You find the 15 percent row in the table on page 123, look to the right and find that today you can pay a P-E ratio of 34.3 and earn an annual return of 10 percent. In fact, General Reinsurance is selling at a P-E ratio of 28.2, *so you will make a return in excess of 10 percent.*

The tables in the previous chapter gave price ranges for the

	1965 High	1970 Low	% Gain (Loss)	Annual Return (Excluding Dividend)
Avon Products	38	59	55.3	9
IBM	179	219	22.3	4
3M	71	71	—	—
Perkin-Elmer	20	18	(10.0)	—
Xerox	72	65	(10.0)	—

shares of these companies in 1965 or 1966 and 1970. Sometimes, as indicated in the table opposite, if one had bought the shares at their 1965 highs and sold at the 1970 lows, one would have lost or made very little money.

If the timing were perfect and the investor had bought at the 1965 low and sold at the 1970 high, the returns would have been spectacular:

	1965 Low	1970 High	% Gain (Loss)	Annual Return (Excluding Dividend)
Avon Products	26	92	253.8	29
IBM	131	387	195.4	24
3M	54	115	113.0	16
Perkin-Elmer	12	46	283.3	30
Xerox	32	116	262.5	29

The trick is to end up somewhere in between most of the time. We believe the techniques described in this chapter should be helpful to that end.

10

How to Invest in Problem Companies

The great majority of publicly owned companies in the United States are in some kind of trouble. Some of them—whose problems are temporary and can be solved—represent excellent value. Others do not.

As already indicated (hopefully not to the point of reader exhaustion), it takes a special combination of managerial, technical, and marketing skills for a company to rise above the general battle, to create and dominate large, new markets that provide continually handsome returns for shareholders. (In recent years approximately sixty companies have accounted for close to half of all domestic corporate profits. Eight companies have accounted for nearly a quarter of the total.)

Nevertheless, there is money to be made in problem companies. There is a place for them in a portfolio.

As an investor in a problem company, *your* problem is to distinguish between those concerns that have a genuine recovery potential and those in which present difficulties will persist. Most businessmen—including company presidents—must be optimistic about their company's future. How else can they summon the energy to go to the office every day and to devote more time to their careers than to any other aspect of their lives? This optimism, this "can do" approach, is one of the important reasons that we have a trillion-dollar economy. But as an investor you must beware of false managerial hopes sometimes buttressed, alas, by the superficial and naïve judgments of investment advisers and brokers.

Keep the following investment principles in mind when considering a commitment in a problem company:

1. Every investment in a problem or value company (as opposed to a growth company) requires *two* decisions: when to *buy* and when to *sell*. Rarely does this kind of company turn into the kind of success story we have been describing, the kind of money tree you can hold and shake for a decade or more.

2. Patience may be even more necessary for the owner of a problem company than of a growth stock. Admittedly, the growth stocks we discuss in this book by and large sell at high price-earnings ratios and provide low dividends. It may take some time before you realize sizable appreciation. However, the problems of problem companies have a way of lingering, almost always postponing rewards longer than one anticipates. "The way out of trouble," according to E. W. Howe, "is never as simple as the way in."

Let us list ten key problems confronting what may euphemistically be described as "nongrowth" companies.

1. *Cyclical problems.* The difficulties of the business cycle affect the great bulk of American companies. Each time the economy slumps, a staggering array of mining and manufacturing concerns —steel, auto, machine tool, paper, housing, chemical companies, etc.—suffer the slings and arrows of idle capacity and price weakness. Earnings drop and dividends are jeopardized.

2. *Regulatory problems.* Utilities, railroads, airlines, banks, insurance companies, broadcasters, investment banking and brokerage firms and others are subject to regulation. Sometimes this creates a degree of certainty; more often, uncertainty. One can never tell, for example, whether rate increases will be granted, route structures changed, or mergers permitted. Long lags may persist between the adjustment of revenues to rising costs. One's political antennae have to be sharply tuned.

3. *Labor problems.* Only about 17 million, or 18 to 19 percent

of our domestic work force of 85 million people, are unionized. Such labor unions have penetrated deeply into a number of basic industries: steel and automobiles, for example. On the whole, managements have not done a good job in standing up to unionized labor because they have believed the increased wages and fringe benefits could be passed on to customers in the form of higher prices. A company with high direct labor costs and strongly entrenched unions faces the recurring difficulties of strikes and strike threats. Both distort earning patterns. Costs increase faster than productivity, and if prices are raised to offset these higher costs, the company usually runs into the next problem.

4. *Import problems.* Find a company with a serious labor problem and you are likely to find an import problem as well. High domestic labor costs have been a prominent factor in the generation of foreign competition in steel, autos, aluminum, chemicals, textiles, and glass, to specify a few areas. There are also American corporations that have been sluggish about keeping their products up to date—insufficiently attuned to consumer styles, needs, and pocketbooks—who have been clobbered by alert Japanese and Western European competitors. This brings us to still another problem.

5. *Obsolescence.* Some companies ride on successful products too long. Then new competition arrives, taking advantage of patent expirations, improved research, or more effective marketing. Such competition destroys the original leader's position of strength. (We will later discuss one such problem company to illustrate the difficulties and opportunities involved in betting on a comeback.)

6. *Technological problems.* We refer here not to the company suffering from product obsolescence but to those experiencing difficulty in converting a new technology into profitable, mass-produced products. Occasionally a concern shifts from one kind of manufacturing process to another and cannot smoothly bring the new line on-stream. New chemical plants, oil refineries, paper mills, and large printing presses are cases in point.

7. *Ecological and environmental problems.* Of all the problems we list, this one is the newest and hardest to evaluate. The environ-

mental problem is having an impact on virtually the whole economy. It has delayed transportation of oil and gas from Alaska, arousing emotions and disturbing corporate earnings patterns. It affects the construction of coal-mining facilities. It hastens the obsolescence of paper mills. It increases the cost of automobiles. More importantly, it casts real doubt on the future growth rates of a number of basic industries. In view of our environmental problems, *can we really consume 50 to 100 percent more electricity per capita in the United States ten years from now, as the electric utilities insist?*

8. *Nationalization problems.* Any company with substantial assets overseas—particularly in less-developed nations—lives with the possibility that such assets will be expropriated. Witness the recent experiences of Kennecott and Anaconda in Chile, or the growing success of the Arab oil-producing nations in obtaining a higher share of profits from oil production, and their demands for an equity position.

9. *Financial problems.* This is a problem in and of itself but tends also to be the end result of all the other difficulties we enumerate. It manifests itself, ultimately, in the form of inadequate cash balances. Borrowing power is exhausted. Convertible securities and warrants adorn the balance sheet like Christmas tree ornaments—bright but empty. Dividends on the company's common stock are omitted, and a low price-earnings ratio makes it difficult, if not impossible, to raise additional equity capital.

If the company is short of cash simply because it has allowed its accounts receivable and inventory to get out of hand, the financial problem in question can often be corrected. But the fact that a company does not have these assets under control tells you something about its management.

10. *Management problems.* Depressed enough? If not, hang on.

If a company has a *nonmanagerial* problem of sufficient severity, the quality of its management may be irrelevant. Take Kennecott Copper. Let's assume it has the best management in the world. The company's large Chilean mines have been expropriated. Its merger with Peabody Coal is being contested by the Justice Department.

The future of its new and proposed Southwestern coal and copper mining facilities is clouded by environmental complications. Its domestic copper-mining and fabricating business is beset by problems of low-grade ore bodies and competition from newer materials. How can a management with all the dedication and intelligence in the world make a situation with these underlying fundamentals attractive to you as an investor *relative to* other investment opportunities?

In a number of other cases, however, *management itself is the problem.* And this is almost always *top* management. In most situations the man at the top, and the associates he selects, still make virtually all the difference.

Telltale signs of management weakness include, but should not be restricted to, the following:

• an aging top executive
• nepotism*
• luxurious executive facilities
• a record of overly optimistic forecasts
• high executive turnover
• too many footnotes to the company financial statements
• lack of clearly defined corporate objectives

We submit that if you test the companies we have described as "successful" in the preceding chapters of this book, *you will find that in an overwhelming number of cases they have none of these problems.* We urge you to measure any other companies you are considering for investment against the list of ten problems to determine whether they are successful or not.

Assuming, as a result of this exercise, that you discover the company in question is a problem company, and you want to consider investing in it on that basis, then proceed as follows:

1. *Define the problems.* Are they external and thus out of management control? Or are they internal, depending more on new

---

* There are exceptions to every rule, and several of the successful companies we describe in this book have been run by one family for several generations.

capital expenditure programs, extensive research efforts, or new marketing programs? Ask yourself and your adviser why the company is in this position and, depending on your answer, how realistic it is to expect it to extricate itself in the near future.

2. *Do not invest in a company with too many problems.* Especially avoid companies that have to cope both with external (say, import) difficulties and with internal weaknesses (lousy management). Many times the two go hand in hand. Sometimes there's a real opportunity when they do *not* go hand in hand.

3. *Avoid companies with a serious financial problem.* Solutions to most of the other difficulties we have described require money —as well as people and time. If a company has borrowed all the money it reasonably can, if it must raise additional common stock at 5 times earnings, and if it can pay no dividend while you wait, our advice is to look elsewhere. What Henry Crown may wish to accomplish personally at General Dynamics (in his second round) or what the Rockefellers may once have been willing to risk on Chrysler or Eastern Airlines is almost certainly not for you.

4. *Avoid companies with management problems.* Life is too short, and there are too many good managements, to risk handing your money over to a bunch of second-raters. The other side of this coin is: *Keep your eye out for situations in which there has been an important, constructive management change at the top.* But in these situations look carefully at the old problems the new management will have to solve and do not be impatient. We know of virtually no situations in which a new management in the last decade has turned a problem company around in less than three years. You may have to wait even longer. But if you can double your money in, say, five years, the wait may be worth it.

5. *Find companies that reward you while you wait.* You should be rewarded by a generous dividend return while awaiting new and improved industry conditions, more effective management, or some combination of the two, to take hold.

6. *Ask yourself whether a less problematical company in a particular industry would not do as well or nearly as well as the particular company you are considering.* Do you, for example,

want to "go all the way" and buy Pan American World Airways, a problem company par excellence, or would you be better advised to invest in TWA? A favorable change in industry conditions will help both, but it may not help Pan Am enough.

In concluding, let's take a brief look at one company that illustrates, *in principle,* the kinds of risks that may be worth taking in that portion of your portfolio devoted to "turnaround" situations. The company is Smith, Kline & French Laboratories.

SKF's management admits that it rode far too long on its successes of the 1950s and 1960s as the developer, patenter, and marketer of Thorazene and a host of other tranquilizers. For years the company as a whole was overstaffed and its research efforts superficial, undermanned, and inadequately funded.

As Thorazene patents expired, and as the Justice Department and the Food & Drug Administration restricted the sale of amphetamines, and as no compensating new products materialized, SKF stock, which had commanded a premium price-earnings ratio, plunged from a high of 86¾ in 1965 to a low of 36 in 1969. The value now given it *in relation to other drug companies* is dramatically illustrated in the following two tables:

Smith, Kline & French vs. Other Drug Industry Securities— Comparative Analysis

	Market Value in Millions of Dollars*	Net Sales per Share†	Net Sales per Dollar of Market Value†	Net Earnings Before Taxes as % of Sales†
Smith, Kline & French	$ 838	$23.70	$0.41	23
Eli Lilly	3,871	8.70	0.15	25
Merck	4,520	20.51	0.17	29
Warner-Lambert	3,058	32.77	0.41	15
Upjohn	1,071	27.02	0.37	19
G. D. Searle	1,086‡	13.50	0.19	16

* *Based on shares outstanding at year end 1970, stock prices as of 12/31/71.*
† *Based on 1970 results.*
‡ *Assuming full dilution of Cumulative Convertible Preferred Stock.*

Drug Industry—Comparative Analysis

	Current Price 12/31/71	Earnings per Share†				Price-Earnings Ratio			Current Indicated Dividend	Current Yield—%
		1969	1970	1971*	1972*	1970	1971*	1972*		
Smith, Kline & French	57	$2.81	$3.01	$3.10	$3.35	19.0X	18.5X	17.1X	$2.00	3.5
Eli Lilly	57	1.26	1.40	1.35	1.65	40.6	42.1	34.5	0.70	1.2
Merck	124	2.80	3.11	3.45	3.95	39.9	35.9	31.4	2.20	1.8
Warner-Lambert	80	2.39	2.57	2.80	3.05	31.0	28.5	26.1	1.30	1.6
Upjohn	73	2.54	2.56	2.65	3.00	28.4	27.5	24.3	1.60	2.2
G. D. Searle	74	2.08	2.32	2.60	2.80	31.8	28.4	26.3	1.30	1.8

* Estimated.
† All earnings-per-share figures are based on the Faulkner, Dawkins & Sullivan Universe, "Comparative Summary of Earnings and Market Performance," October 29, 1971.

Under the supervision of a new president, Tom Rauch, in his late forties, the company began several years ago to plan for the next two decades. Management recognized that it would take many years to rebuild the company from the ground up and determined to do so carefully and unflamboyantly. It has increased its commitment to pharmaceutical research. It has embarked on a program of building its lines of proprietary consumer products, which it hopes will ultimately represent 50 percent of its net income. In an unusual statement of corporate objectives, management stated that the company's goal is "to attain annual earnings increases of 10% or more. We realize, however, that in the next few years a more modest target is required as we continue to invest in projects for the long run."

Here, then, is a sound industry environment (the best companies in the drug industry do very well indeed); a management that candidly recognizes past mistakes and is moving to correct them (but is not promising the moon in the process); a stock price which is still skeptical about the future; and a dividend return which, if not spectacular, is somewhat better than average and is well protected.

These are a few of the ingredients required to make a rewarding investment in a problem company. Whether *this* problem company proves rewarding or not remains to be seen.

IMPLEMENTATION

11

How to Choose a Broker
or Investment Adviser

LIKE your doctor or lawyer, your broker or investment adviser must be someone in whom you have complete trust. He treats your financial security with the same consideration and in the same confidence that your doctor does when he advises you on matters of personal health, and your lawyer when he attends to your legal affairs.

Events of the late sixties have impressed on all of us the need for care in the selection of a broker. During the great "back-office crunch" of 1968–1970, more than a hundred member firms of the New York Stock Exchange merged or were liquidated, either voluntarily or otherwise. Some of the historic firms of the investment business, with thousands of individual clients throughout the country, disappeared in the worst brokerage crisis in Wall Street's history. Although we know of no individual investor who has suffered permanent personal financial loss attributable to back-office difficulties at these member firms, many persons were frightened by the long delays in the receipt of their securities and cash, by deteriorating service, by the rumors and stories of administrative chaos, and by the general disarray that accompanied the demise of these firms.

The consequences of the convulsion of 1968–1970 will be a

series of legislative and regulatory reforms of which only the earliest have emerged as we complete this book.

The first of these measures was the passage by Congress in the closing months of 1970 of the Securities Investor Protection Corporation, SIPC, a nonprofit corporation that insures each customer's claims for assets held by a brokerage house for up to $50,000. Assessments on each broker-dealer member provide the basic funds, with up to $1 billion of reserves available from a standby line of credit with the U.S. Treasury Department. Losses due to poor investment selection are not covered.

Under the active direction of the new SEC Chairman, William J. Casey, a whole series of stricter regulations for supervision of the securities industry—covering the transfer of securities purchased and sold, the segregation of excess cash reserves held for clients by brokerage houses, the reliability and completeness of information divulged by corporations, and the quality of research recommendations made available to the public—have been proposed by the SEC and, in our judgment, will gradually be promulgated by that organization or legislated by Congress. If effected, the changes in the securities industry, designed to protect the 31 million shareholders of American industry from unsound practices, will be profound.

In order to be an effective investor you need continuing professional advice. Such help can come from a number of sources. Larger accounts can call upon the services of counseling firms—registered under the Investment Advisers' Act of 1940—which offer investment advice to clients of all kinds. Under this act any adviser who has more than fourteen clients must be registered with the SEC. In recent years there has been a proliferation of such firms offering their services to both private and institutional clients. Generally, they have a minimum account size, which has lately escalated to the $500,000 level, although some firms have imposed even stiffer minimum-account-size requirements.

These investment counseling organizations are located throughout the country. The larger ones maintain regional offices in major financial centers. Counseling begins with a discussion of your overall financial position, and includes overall investment strategy, estate planning, and generational considerations, as well as advice on specific securities. Your investments are appraised periodically —usually quarterly, but not always so—in writing and in person. Compensation is usually based on a percentage of the assets under supervision. A sliding scale is normal, with the percentage declining as the sum of the account under management increases. The traditional base fee has been one-half of 1 percent of assets under supervision, but the newer counseling firms, operating with smaller total-asset bases, tend to charge more. All fees paid for investment advice are tax-deductible under the Internal Revenue Code.

You can give these firms complete discretion over the assets you have assigned to them to supervise, in which case they have the right to buy and sell securities without consulting you, or you can reserve the prerogative of making the decision yourself, utilizing your counselor strictly in an advisory capacity. While most of the newer counseling organizations prefer the former method (it simplifies their communications and their decision-making time, and also tends to improve their transaction-executing ability and investment timing), since this book is designed to help private investors learn how to make their own investment selections, most of our readers may prefer to retain the final investment decision for themselves. Fees for discretionary and nondiscretionary accounts are usually the same, although not always, since more work accompanies a nondiscretionary account.

Almost all the major counseling firms—such as Stein, Roe & Farnham and Scudder, Stevens & Clark—and the newer groups —such as Brokaw, Schaenen, Clancy & Co. and Davis, Palmer & Biggs—are not affiliated with brokerage firms. Two of the oldest and best-known firms have been taken over in recent years—Lionel D. Edie & Company by Merrill Lynch; and Loomis, Sayles by the New England Mutual Life Insurance Company. The primary advantages of nonaffiliation are the ability to make investment judgments independent of any brokerage revenue consideration, and the flexibility that it permits in the use of a broker to obtain good execution of customers' orders. These firms parcel out their orders to brokerage firms based on: (1) the quality of research received therefrom; (2) the skill demonstrated by the brokers in executing orders; and (3) instructions from clients to direct business to specific brokers.

A number of brokers and investment bankers have themselves formed investment counseling departments under the Investment Advisers' Act of 1940. Although they find themselves in the anomalous role of competing against their customers (the counseling firms that direct brokerage business to others), these firms also provide sound investment services. Some of them offset commissions against investment counseling fees, which appears to be a client cost advantage, although it raises the question of a possible conflict of interest.

These complex interrelationships are part of the problem of "institutional access," which has aroused such controversy within the securities business. Some previously independent counselors have acquired memberships on regional securities exchanges, some have preserved complete separation of function, but all anticipate forthcoming changes as rulings are issued by the SEC on negotiated commissions and on the matter of whether institutions can belong to various security exchanges.

In addition to investment counseling firms, investors can receive advice from banks, which not only manage trusts but handle money on an "agency" basis in their own investment counseling departments, in a manner analogous to the independent firms. The Boston Company, bank-holding-company parent of the Boston Safe Deposit Company, a traditional trust bank, has acquired a group of independent counseling firms around the nation, from Seattle and San Francisco to New York City, in an effort to build a nationwide counseling service. Subscription services such as Standard & Poor's have beefed up their fee-based investment counseling organizations through joint ventures with independent groups, hoping thus to obtain talented personnel and to create incentives for those people.

Finally, you can choose among the myriad closed-end and open-end investment trusts, or utilize any number of general or specialized bank-run common trust funds. In all such cases, your investment decisions are made for you. The major investment counseling services—including Stein, Roe; Scudder; and Loomis, Sayles —also offer a variety of no-load mutual funds, as do some investment banking firms.

For the great majority of investors, a broker is the obvious and most practical source of help. A broker may be someone who acts as "agent" when buying and selling a security, functioning only as a middleman; he may be a broker-dealer, who, in addition to acting as agent, takes a position in stocks and sells them to clients out of inventory as "principal"; or he may be an investment banker whose primary function is to "float" new issues to the public. Most likely he is a combination of all three, particularly if he represents a major organization, or even if he works for one of the many regional brokerage firms that function throughout our country.

You don't have to have a great deal of money to use a broker. There is no minimum capital requirement, as with most investment counselors and banks, but a good broker will ask you certain questions about your credit standing, including the name of your local bank, and will require assurance of the availability of funds before opening an account for you. The compensation you pay a broker is the commission that is charged when securities are bought and sold. Depending on the firm he represents, he may receive a percentage of the gross commission, or he may receive a salary, with incentives related to his total commission business. In the case of stocks listed on the various exchanges, these commissions are fixed (until the dollar volume of a single transaction for a single customer exceeds $500,000).* With an over-the-

* All told, it will cost you—in commissions and miscellaneous taxes— approximately 1 percent of your investment to buy 100 shares of common stock at 50. If you change your mind, sell the stock, and invest $5,000 in

counter security, where the broker-dealer acts as principal, the charge is not fixed, but should not differ appreciably from a commission for a listed stock. If you buy shares on a "net" basis, with the commission included in the price of the shares, the broker-dealer must disclose to you that he is acting as principal on your notice of purchase or sale. An investment banker selling a new issue can do so only by means of a prospectus, a detailed document describing the nature and record of the company in question, which must be approved beforehand by the SEC in Washington.

What questions should you ask if you are choosing a broker, or if you are ascertaining the financial characteristics of your present or a prospective new broker? And of whom should you ask them?

Usually, brokers are found through word of mouth: a relative or friend recommends his. However, your choice should be based on ability, not on a low golf handicap or tennis partnership. How do you verify his or her merits? Generally, you hear only about the good things, not the bad, because few investors ever admit they are not doing well in the market. Your best bets are your local bank, your lawyer, and your accountant. All these sources should have access to information about the reputation of the firm and the broker you have in mind, or ways to develop such information. A bank is a particularly useful reference point, for it serves brokerage firms in a number of different ways: it lends them money, it holds their deposits, and, if it has a trust department, it may receive research material, and be knowledgeable about their ability to transact orders.

Find out if the firm involved is a member of the New York Stock Exchange, or of a regional exchange. Does it belong to the National Association of Security Dealers? Find out if it is registered with the SEC. All these agencies require that their member firms file detailed financial data with them. If you have any questions about

---

another issue, you will be out of pocket 3 percent of your initial investment. This is not insignificant in relation to your annual goal of a 10 to 12 percent return. It argues for choosing individual issues carefully and sticking with them.

firms or registered representatives, you can write to these organizations or ascertain the financial condition of the firm in question (all NYSE member firms must publish independently audited, annual balance sheets), and the state of an individual broker's clearance. All partners, officers, and registered representatives are required to take both New York Stock Exchange and NASD examinations to test their knowledge and competency before they are authorized to practice their profession. The recent "back-office crunch" has produced more stringent supervision and emphasis on compliance with Exchange regulations by member firms. All member firms of the New York Stock Exchange operate "compliance" departments, which include trained legal and auditing personnel for the protection both of clients and of the firms themselves from any violations of regulations.

If by chance you receive mail which solicits your securities business from an organization whose name you do not know, be sure that it is registered with the SEC. No broker-dealer or investment banker can use the mails if he is not registered with the SEC. To be sure, there are eminent firms that do not belong to the New York or American Stock Exchanges, or even the regional exchanges, although they should be members of the NASD. Nonmembership on an exchange has no bearing on integrity or ability. A firm dealing only in mutual funds or in over-the-counter issues need not belong to an exchange, although, as we have said, it must be registered with the NASD.

There are enough fine investment firms in this country to make it unnecessary for you to end up in the hands of unreliable operators selling suspect merchandise. *There is no substitute for integrity and competence.* Be sure that the firm and the individual member from whom you are planning to seek such advice are reputable members of your community; be sure that they fall under the regulatory agencies; and above all, make certain of their financial condition.

When studying the financial pages of the newspapers to learn more about a prospective brokerage firm, look for the firm that avoids extravagant promises, fancy jargon, long lists of hot pros-

pects, and dramatics. The New York Stock Exchange rigidly controls the advertising of all its member firms. It requires advance
approval by its Department of Public Relations of all advertising
for newspapers, magazines, radio, and TV. The tone of the advertising must be soft-sell and educational in approach, dignified
and not overpowering.

On the other hand, there are some advisory services whose advertising in various financial publications is blatant, stupid, and
sometimes downright silly.

Advertising should not be the primary reason for selecting an
advisory organization, but it may help you to understand the nature
of the organization. It may help you to know more about its special
qualifications, its emphasis on research services or retail sales, mutual funds, or other aspects of the investment world.

The quality of a firm's research is of fundamental importance to
your investment program. Many firms boast of their research activities. "Research in depth" has become a popular, almost universal
calling card. The activity of some firms that cull the weekly reports
of publications and advisory services may have some merit, but it
should not be confused with primary research, conducted by experienced security analysts who go out into the field to visit company managements, and who make comparative corporate and
industry analyses. Some firms have highly specialized but limited
research capabilities, others possess a broader scope. The specialist
research organization that follows the railroad industry in depth has
a role to play, but your investment success will usually depend on
access to information about a broad range of growth companies
more than an in-depth knowledge of a particular industry.

Many regional firms do excellent research into major companies
located nearby, and rely for their overall perspective on research
provided by a correspondent house, and/or from special research
organizations such as Argus Research.* While not ideal, this

---

* Argus Research has a high reputation for the quality and continuity of
its efforts.

secondhand approach is a great deal better than no access to research at all.

In the course of your investigation, a study of the brokerage house's latest research material is perfectly in order. Check carefully to see if it can be categorized as (1) short, slapdash, and superficial or (2) lengthy, almost wholly descriptive, and tedious. What you need is something in between—*not length but interpretation and insights,* and simple, appropriate documentation.

Does the brokerage report in question weigh the risks of a given investment against the rewards? Are any negatives mentioned, or are they overlooked? Does the report grapple with the fundamentals or is it simply a string of optimistic generalizations?

The most vital ingredient in your decision-making is the individual who will act as your representative. The chemistry between you must be right. It takes a long time to get to know each other well, so that he will anticipate your needs and your problems, and so that you will understand his approach. You must be able to communicate with each other. A reasonable trade-off must be established between his interest in a long-term relationship with you and your willingness to respect the fact that he has other clients to look after and a limited amount of time to give any one of them.

When you are developing a long-range investment program (which we believe is the proper approach for our readers), you probably don't want someone who sells only "new issues." Nor do you want someone who is interested only in speculative situations —what people refer to as "home runs." Be sure that the registered representative can think for himself. If he only mirrors the words of his organization without interpreting them to meet your individual personal needs, you will be asking for trouble. Neither do you want the registered representative who ignores or denigrates the research work of his organization and utilizes only his own ideas, which may or may not have received his firm's approval.

How much experience should your investment adviser have? If he is young, and learning, but intelligent, sensitive, adaptable, and respected in his organization, he will value you as a client, and you can grow together. The combination can be ideal. You are valuable to each other. But you have to be prepared for the fact that he will make mistakes.

Do you want an older broker? If he is successful, he already has many clients and may not pay sufficient attention to you. Like many customers' men who began many years ago, he may not have made the transition to the good but newer companies which should comprise part of the portfolio you are constructing. You may well get off to a good start with an experienced broker but then be faced with a search for a replacement when he retires to take life easier.

However you choose, both of you will have to exercise patience. Investing is a learning experience. No two clients are alike. Not every recommendation will work out the way it is planned. It will be more important for you to review in your mind after six months, and again and again as time progresses, whether your adviser is meeting your criteria. Is he or she more than a glorified order-taker? Is he acting as a sounding board for ideas? Is he initiating ideas from his research department that conform to your needs? Does he have a balanced view of investing or is he only interested in commissions? Does he respond to your needs, and at all times keep you informed? If so, then you and he have a leg up on the development of your long-term investment strategy and the construction of a profitable portfolio.

12

What to Talk About with Your Broker

W HAT kinds of questions should I ask my broker? How do I keep him on his toes after he has made his initial investments for me? The dialogue must be maintained to make the relationship work. Presumably you have satisfied yourself about his background and qualifications or you wouldn't be using his services.

The following checklist may help:

1. *Does your broker answer your questions?* Why isn't a particular stock behaving as expected? Has a particular stock, especially a problem company which has straightened out, met your objectives? What is happening in the race between Polaroid and Kodak to develop the next generation of in-process instant cameras and films? What does the change in capital-gains tax rates mean to you? What are the ramifications of RCA's withdrawal from the computer business, and how are the merged computer operations of GE and Honeywell doing? What is the significance of an acquisition, a corporate official's death, or a Supreme Court antitrust decision?

Your broker may not answer all these questions himself. He should have some of the answers, and enlist the support of his research personnel to answer the rest. When he doesn't know the answer, he should say so, not try to "cuff" it.

Don't expect an answer to *every* question; your broker is a broker, not a Svengali.

2. *Does he keep you posted?* You must be kept up to date on your investments and alternatives, even though you are not thinking of making any changes in your holdings. Most good investors will tell you that it is more important to know what is happening to the investments you own than to the stocks you are thinking of buying.

Possibly, if you are actively engaged in your investments and sustain a continuing dialogue, you will be fully informed at all times. If you are interested but too busy to keep in constant touch, your broker should call you from time to time to bring you up to date and to suggest possible changes. One of the reasons you have gone to him is because you are busy with your own business. You depend on his initiative.

When you buy shares in a company because it meets your investment criteria, and because you believe your broker is well informed about its prospects, you have a right to expect that he will also keep you informed, and not *forget* that you own the stock. We reiterate the importance of this when companies are having problems. Problems are to be faced, understood, and evaluated, not to be ignored. You shouldn't have to learn of your triumphs from your broker, and your disasters from the newspapers.

3. *Does he make appropriate suggestions?* Is your adviser following the investment philosophy upon which you agreed initially? *Does he agree with you about the five characteristics of the enduringly successful company we have discussed in this book, and is he on the lookout for emerging companies that have these qualities?*

Is he substituting so-called "inside information" for sound reasoning, or gambles—say, a new oil discovery—for basic developments? Is he buying new and unseasoned issues when your needs are for conservative, moderate-growth objectives? Is he using too many securities in your account relative to its size? If you believe any or all of these situations are occurring, then you had better remind your broker of your objectives. You must not hesitate to remind him of your objectives and investment philosophy.

4. *Does he churn your account?* "Churn" is one of the more delightfully descriptive terms in the Wall Street lexicon. It refers to the process of moving your account around, of buying a stock one day and selling it the next—buying, selling, buying, selling, buying, selling, until your broker's pockets are filled with commissions and your heart with despair.

If you have done your investigating thoroughly beforehand, and your broker works for a reputable firm, the chances of this happening are, by definition, remote. The compliance departments of Exchange member firms, making good use of the computer installations that can observe activity in accounts, scrutinize daily trading carefully to spot any signs of churning.

5. *Does he alibi?* The best investment men in the world make mistakes. Is your broker one of those people who always blames the other fellow—the analyst, the company president, the market? If a stock fails to work out as planned after a suitable time has elapsed, does he hang on, assuring you that success is just around the corner, or is he willing to admit he made a mistake and move on to more promising opportunities? Bernard Baruch, a most successful investor, had a policy of admitting his errors promptly, and allowing his successes to run.

Now, in all fairness to your broker or adviser, we should point out a few ways *not* to keep him on his toes:

1. *Don't try to chisel.* Unless you are a trader, interested in a short-term profit, don't try to squeeze out each eighth of a point when you are buying a stock. If you are a long-term investor, buying a stock for fundamental reasons, with plans to accumulate additional shares gradually, on an informal dollar-averaging* basis,

* Dollar-averaging means purchasing a fixed dollar amount of a given security at regular intervals—say, monthly. As a stock goes up, a fixed dollar purchase buys fewer shares; as it goes down, the same investment buys more shares. The purpose of this approach—which is a useful way of solving the timing problems described in Chapter 9—is to help you purchase your position in a particular stock at a reasonable average price over time.

buy the stock. Limit orders can be masterminded by professionals managing money on a discretionary basis, or may be used if you believe a stock has reasons to decline significantly, and should then be bought. If you are going away, and believe that a stock may reach a realistic buy or sell price, limit orders can be used to implement your investment program. The long-term investor should not be overly concerned that a stock or stocks may "sell off a little."

2. *Don't be a crybaby.* If a stock declines after you buy it, or goes up after you sell it, don't assume automatically that it is the broker's fault. If you have given an adviser discretion to manage your account, then he must be man enough to shoulder responsibility for its achievements, or lack thereof, after a specific time period (two to three years). If you are working with your broker on the type of joint-venture basis we have described, you and your broker must share responsibility. If a stock you have both selected moves lower, and you begin to criticize, you may inhibit his future suggestions by making him so wary that you will miss your opportunity to buy more of the issue at an appropriate time, or he will play it so safe that you will end up with a mediocre portfolio, thus minimizing the opportunity for gain as well as the possibility of loss.

3. *Don't be a know-it-all.* Many investors have a reflex action when their broker or counselor gives them a new idea. They say (or think): "My idea is better. That product is no good. I didn't like its taste." We recommend that in order to maximize your opportunities you greet the suggestions of your professional helpers with an open mind, evaluating them in the light of their appropriateness to your particular objectives, recognizing that your taste, judgment, etc., may not reflect a majority view or acceptance of a product.

Furthermore, give your broker a little credit when stocks go up. He probably dies a thousand deaths when they go down; he is entitled to compensating joy when they appreciate, even if the credit is partly yours.

4. *Don't ask your broker or adviser to do your income-tax returns.* It's not his job.

5. *Don't overuse your broker's time and services.* If you monop-

olize your adviser's time with petty questions and reviews, asking him too often for quotes on stocks during the day (which you will find in the newspaper that day or the next), you will irritate and antagonize him, and may not be the recipient of his attention and thought when it is really important. Remember that a broker or adviser, particularly a good one (whom we presume you have selected), must share you with other clients.

6. *Ask sensible questions.* Don't waste time with nonessential questions, tips having to do with mergers, dividend increases, stock splits, impending contract awards, and heaven knows what else. Like other time-consuming talk, such conversation, frequently engaged in to give an appearance of sophistication, only detracts from concentration on such matters as the five requisites to corporate success, or the ten corporate problems described in Chapter 10. It is a waste of time.

Remember, above all, that a broker-adviser–client relationship blooms slowly, that impatience may distort the relationship, and that the ultimate proof of success comes only with time.

13

The Final Step:
Organizing Your Portfolio

THERE once was a trader on the floor of the New York Stock Exchange who had a weekly Tuesday morning appointment with his barber. On his way to the barbershop he passed the post at which Penn Central was traded. Each week he purchased 100 shares of Penn Central on his way to the barber and on his return he sold the stock, thus for a number of years financing his haircuts. One morning while he was in the chair the broad tape told the story of a terrible storm that was expected to cause Penn Central severe loss. By the time the trader returned from having his locks shorn, Penn Central stock was trading much lower, and he had lost the cost of many haircuts. Recognizing the virtue of flexibility, he changed his strategy. Henceforth, if it was raining while he was on his way to his haircut he sold 100 shares of Penn Central short and purchased 100 shares of Book-of-the-Month Club. He reasoned that if it was sufficiently stormy outside to hurt the railroad, a number of people would stay home to read and this would help the Book-of-the-Month Club.

Then there was the man who listened to the nicknames of companies on the New York Stock Exchange. (It has long been the custom of brokers to give companies nicknames based upon their Exchange symbols.) Several years ago two of the more active securities listed on the Exchange were U.S. Hoffman Machinery

152

(symbol HMY), nicknamed Hymie, and Amphenol Borg (symbol ABE), nicknamed Abie. If this portfolio strategist saw that Hymie was strong, he bought Abie. He felt that Hymie and Abie went together.

So far in this book we have talked about (1) setting overall investment objectives; (2) defining your investment philosophy; (3) selecting individual stocks; and (4) finding and using a financial adviser. The way in which you put this all together into a portfolio of common stocks is the last element of an effective investment strategy. Our recommendations for putting your portfolio together may not be as colorful as those of the traders we have just described, but we think the following simple rules work.

First: *Don't start by putting all your money into common stocks.* If you have all of your money in them now, take some out.

It's impossible to tell you exactly how much of your liquid resources should be in the market at any given time. A precise figure depends on the amount of risk you are willing to take: your annual spending in relation to your annual salary, your outstanding liabilities, your prospects. Much also depends on your emotional stability. Are you cool or do you panic in times of stock market crisis? How did you react when the stock market last took a drubbing and your stocks behaved like so many dying swans? We recommend that you apply the "sleep at night" rule to determine how much *not* to invest: *Keep enough cash uninvested so that you don't lie awake wondering if you've really got enough.*

If you put 50 percent of your liquid assets into stocks and the market goes down 20 percent (it dropped 36 percent from the 1969 high to the 1970 low, the sharpest drop since World War II), you will have lost 10 percent of your liquid funds. This isn't pleasant, but you shouldn't hit the panic button and sell at the bottom.

Investors often succumb to the powerful tendency, as stock markets move up, to become more fully invested, with the result that the typical individual investor (and institution, too) ends up with all his money committed at the wrong time. When the future appears brightest, accidents invariably happen. In 1962 the market dropped not because general economic conditions worsened but because investors temporarily lost confidence. In more recent years widespread fears about inflation, about war, about "liquidity crises," about the solvency of Wall Street itself, and about international monetary problems have illustrated the sensitivity of stock prices to surprise.

As such surprises come along, a little cash in the bank gives you an emotional as well as a contingency reserve.

The next rule in your investment strategy is: *Don't try to guess the market.*

We have just finished saying that you should make allowances for fluctuations in the market. This is quite different from trying to predict exactly what the market will do and when. Too many amateurs spend too much time trying to figure out whether the market is too high or too low, whether its next big move is up or down. We sympathize with this desire but despair of its success. Most professional investors will confess their difficulty in predicting the general level of stock prices.

With these first two strategic rules, we hope to help you avoid two common mistakes that humiliate the novice investor. The first involves a quick and total plunge into the market. The investor commits his entire nest egg to a group of stocks and then rushes for the evening paper to see how much money he made that day. He suffers from an "I've got to make up for lost time" compulsion. The market immediately goes down, his particular stocks go down with it, and he finds himself 10 to 20 percent in the hole before he's had a chance to catch his breath. He feels foolish, and, in terms of what he can do next, he is helpless.

The second investor states categorically that he likes this or that stock but the market is too high. He has the wisdom of Jove, the foresight of Cassandra (usually in the form of a terrific chart service), and he is going to sit on the sidelines. Of course, the market immediately moves up, his pet stock moves right along with it, and he stays on the sidelines in a state of psychological paralysis. Now the market is *much* too high, even his old favorite is too high, and he never does take the plunge.

Perhaps the second strategic rule should be regarded as a corollary of the first. Instead of *Don't try to guess the market,* you might express it as *Get your feet wet now.*

Most investors are like O. Henry's "mixture of fools and angels —they rush in and fear to tread at the same time." You want to avoid the agony of impulsive, premature commitment, the heartbreak of overcommitment, and the frustration of noncommitment. You can do this only by easing into the market. You are engaged in a long-term endeavor. By taking your time, by making a partial commitment in a particular stock now and buying the rest later, you are in effect taking the market-guessing out of your decision. If the market goes down, you buy more—providing, always, that you can objectively persuade yourself that the underlying corporate fundamentals are still favorable. You end up with a reasonable average cost. If the market goes up, you will have a profit under your belt, you will feel pretty clever, and you will add to your holdings—provided, again, that you can satisfy yourself that the fundamentals are still there. Again, you should end up with a reasonable average cost.

This may not seem particularly courageous. We would rather have you save your courage for the crucial job of stock selection. You would be amazed at how many investors make a bold selection—pick a stock that would be an outstanding investment—and then lose confidence in the stock and in themselves because they bought too much too soon and it went down or they bought none at all and it went up.

Rule three: *Don't buy too many stocks.*

This is an old chestnut, the value of which we have come to appreciate increasingly in recent years. It works. Cut down the number of stocks you own, and your performance will improve.

Gerald Loeb, a well-known broker and financial commentator, is the most famous proponent of this theory. As he puts it in his book *The Battle for Investment Survival,* "The greatest safety lies in putting all your eggs in one basket and watching the basket."

We don't think you should really put all your eggs in one basket (and, of course, neither did he), but we do believe the number of issues should be limited. Five or six will do when you are investing less than $100,000. Between $100,000 and $1 million, you may gradually increase the number to ten to twelve issues.

The fewer companies on your list, the easier it will be to keep track of what you own. You will more quickly identify changes, good or bad, in the fortunes of the corporations involved. Your broker or financial adviser will have the same advantage. You will both make fewer mistakes.

The fewer stocks you permit yourself to buy, the more discipline you will exercise in selecting them. You will cast a more critical eye at a new name if you know that you will have to sell one of your existing holdings in order to buy it. As a result, you will avoid the common error of purchasing every hot tip that comes along. Over the long run, you will own those companies in which you have the greatest continuing confidence, and in so doing you should make the greatest amount of money.

Traditionalists will insist that a broadly diversified list of securities provides greater downside protection than a portfolio that is highly concentrated. If this is true, then it follows that the broadly diversified list limits your upside potential as well.

In actual practice, many diversified lists are less diversified than they seem, offer less protection, and provide less exposure to capital gains than you probably realize. Many typical institutional lists include dozens (sometimes hundreds) of common stocks— three autos, four or five nonferrous metals, seven or eight steels, eight chemicals, a dozen banks, *two* dozen electric utilities. Not surprisingly, a number of these issues (particularly those in the basic, cyclical industries) go up and down together. Not surprisingly, the performance of the portfolio is about average. The diversification provides some protection, but primarily it provides investment officers with an excuse for not making up their minds.

Billy Rose once summed up the hazards of overdiversification as follows: "You got a harem of seventy girls, you don't get to know any of them very well."

If you crave diversification, you should seek not the conventional diversification that calls for having a position in most major companies in most major industries but two other, more unorthodox but effective kinds: (1) time diversification and (2) psychological diversification.

Time diversification simply means that you hold a group of stocks with the expectation that certain of them will provide you with desired returns quickly—within six months to a year—and others with less immediate returns but greater *ultimate* returns over a longer period of time—say, three to five years.

As an illustration, a hypothetical two-stock portfolio might consist of investments in Weyerhaeuser and Eli Lilly. In the case of Weyerhaeuser you reason that a strong recovery in the residential housing industry will bring about a firming of timber and plywood prices, and that the cyclical improvements in the general economy will cause a firming of paper-product prices. Strengthened prices and increased demand will be translated into sharply higher earnings. In turn, these benefits will be reflected in climbing stock prices in the coming months. If it does, you will sell the stock because you still believe that housing and forest-products industries are inherently volatile.

Your cyclical selection will be balanced by a situation where the near-term outlook, while excellent, is already clearly identified, but where the long-term earnings growth is sufficiently bright to assure you of a 10 to 12 percent average annual return over a period of years. Such an example could be Eli Lilly, or it could be ARA Services. In the former instance, although the promising near-term expectations are well defined, and reflected in the price of the stock, the probability of continued rising demand for Lilly's pharmaceutical products throughout the free world, of new drug product introductions stemming from its research activities, and growth in its animal husbandry and agricultural products will produce a rising stream of future earnings. ARA Services will achieve the same growth through the continuing extension of its institutional food services.

Since you do not know when the best time will be to buy these stocks, and since you are convinced of the long-term fundamentals, you buy some shares now. Later you will buy more—and you may even switch your Weyerhaeuser into one of these other investments.

(We repeat: the examples are hypothetical.)

As for *psychological* diversification, we have already referred to the bear market of 1970, to the market peaks of 1966 and 1962, and the extent to which they resulted from change in investor attitudes as well as deterioration in economic fundamentals. Within a given market, individual stocks or groups of stocks can become extraordinarily popular and then, in a twinkling, fall from grace. Similarly, other groups can drift along and then move suddenly into the limelight.

In 1968 certain major oil companies, both international and domestic, participated in important oil discoveries near Prudhoe Bay in Alaska. The market quickly exploited these exploration developments, putting premium price-earnings ratios on these companies, whether international, such as Standard Oil of New Jersey and Mobil Oil, or principally domestic, such as Atlantic Richfield or Standard Oil of Ohio. In its exuberance, the market paid no attention to the problems inherent in the industry. When it became apparent that a combination of circumstances—national concern over environmental protection of the region, rising taxes on Middle East production, discovery disappointments elsewhere—might delay spectacular earnings growth, the stock market did an abrupt about-face: Standard Oil of New Jersey declined from 85 in 1969 to 45 at the beginning of 1970. Mobil dropped from 69 to 36, and Atlantic Richfield from 140 to 50 as anticipated earnings gains were deferred or reduced. While all stocks have recovered, they have not reached their previous highs, and the problems that caused the decline are still unresolved.

Attitudinal changes were more important in these market swings than actual changes in the earnings of these companies. There were no changes in the companies' dividends. In some instances (with both Jersey and Mobil, for example) there were increases in the dividends during the period of decline. Simply stated: A willingness to believe good news was replaced by a willingness both to disbelieve the good and to believe the bad.

Often you will find that the same stocks provide both time *and* psychological diversification. The issue you buy for a relatively quick recovery over the next six to twelve months—as opposed to one you hold for steady, above-average growth over the next three to five years—may well be a depressed, unpopular stock subject to entirely different psychological forces for the long term. This has been the case recently with such depressed securities as Gulf & Western versus Eli Lilly and ARA Services, or American or United Airlines versus Procter & Gamble.

These concepts of diversification make more sense to us than the orthodox, mechanistic, and traditional practice of scattering one's shots—10 percent in chemicals, 10 percent in papers, 5 percent in rubbers, and so forth.

In any event, keep the number of stocks in your portfolio down.

The fourth rule is: *Don't be too income minded.*

Many investors buy stocks for the wrong reasons: for a current dividend return. If current income is your primary interest in life (and current income is nothing to sneer at, we grant you), put most of your money in something other than common stocks, since many stocks, as we have already seen, provide a lower average return than savings institutions, long-term government or corporate bonds, preferred stocks, Treasuries, and long-term, tax-exempt municipals.

In buying common stocks, you must consider the overall return (the "total return," as pension fund managers call it) that results from a combination of dividends and capital appreciation. Taxes on capital gains are lower than on income; so if you are successful in generating gains, you will increase your after-tax profits more than proportionately.

If you reach for stocks that provide unusually high dividend returns (say, 7 to 8 percent in today's market), a perennial temptation to the amateur investor, you are likely to end up with a collection of second-rate companies that provide you with little appreciation and unlimited headache potential. Generalizations of this sort are always dangerous (the exceptions often provide the most interesting investment opportunities), but you can usually assume that the higher the current dividend return provided by an issue: (1) the less interesting are its growth prospects, and (2) the more worried investors are that the dividend will be cut. (Cement, steel, and copper stocks are groups at the moment that provide high returns because investors are unenthusiastic about their long-term earnings prospects.)

The final element of your investment strategy is this: *Know What You Are Trying to Accomplish.*

You must have a specific price objective for every stock you own. And your objective should have a time limit. If your stock fails to meet it, you should ask why. Is it because of general market conditions? Is the company fundamentally less interesting than you had thought? Or is it simply taking other investors longer than you had anticipated to recognize its virtues? Remember that "stubbornness is the energy of fools."

On the other hand, if a stock runs up faster or higher than you had anticipated, you should ask yourself whether new elements have come into the picture that justify the rapid advance and make it still attractive. Or are investors going overboard—buying it simply because it is behaving so well in the market?

Sometimes you may want to continue to hold a stock because you believe other investors will continue to buy it on an emotional basis. This is known as the "greater fool" theory; you are confident that the other person will be sillier than you and that at the moment you want "out" he will still want "in" and will buy your stock. If you do this, don't pretend to yourself that you are holding on because your stock still represents good *value.*

Not all stocks go up right away. Exercise patience. At year end don't overemphasize tax-selling. As each year draws to a close, investors, conscious of a need to offset capital gains, look over their portfolio and choose stocks which are valued at less in the current market than they paid for them, and sell them to reduce their capital gains. More good stocks are sold at the wrong time because investors are trying to minimize taxes, instead of focusing on the undervalued potentials of a good company whose stock is down and is under added pressure at year end because of tax-selling.

Keep your overall objectives in mind, too. Ask yourself whether your individual stock selections are consistent with these objectives. Or are you taking more risk than necessary? After all, you may be able to obtain a satisfactory 10 percent annual return—dividends and capital gains combined—from a high-quality utility stock. If this is your objective (we know everyone wants to make more money than that, but not everyone can afford the risks), why own high-fliers like Memorex or University Computing?

In short, when you buy, when you hold, when you sell, know why you are doing so. Don't get swept up in the emotions of the crowd and make investment decisions out of greed, fright, or the greatest enemy of all, boredom.

CONCLUSION

14

Looking Ahead

W E began this book by reviewing the surprises that influenced securities markets during the last half of the 1960s.

We conclude by hazarding a few predictions about the shape of the 1970s. As investors, we must learn, again and again, to live with complexity and with the unexpected. As we attempt to sort out a mass of conflicting political, social, cultural, and economic factors—all of which converge on, and influence, our financial markets—keep in mind the advice of a wise man, Peter Drucker, who once said: "We know only two things about the future: It cannot be known. It will be different from what exists now and from what we now expect. . . . The best we could hope to do is to anticipate future effects of events which have irrevocably happened."

The Indochina War

We expect it to end. But even if no major conflicts break out elsewhere, we expect defense spending to move up, not down, in response to purported gains in Soviet military capability. While higher in absolute terms, such spending may represent a lower *percent* of total federal spending than during the last ten years.

The National Setting

The two-party system. An important (and much-taken-for-granted) element of stability in American life, it is likely to be under greater pressure in this decade—with the emergence of a huge "independent" vote—than since the election of 1912.

Population growth. Overall, it will be about the same in the 1970s as in the 1960s (23–25 million more people). But the increase in the population of "work-force" age will be far greater, and particularly in the 20-to-45-year-old bracket. Here we can expect an increase of 19 million people in the next decade versus 7 million in the last ten years. There was considerable concern at the beginning of the 1960s about how we were going to be able to absorb population increases into the work force; by comparison with what faces us today the problem then was minor. This indeed is a future event of the sort Drucker describes: The population increase will take place—barring plague, general war, or other calamity—because of events that have "irrevocably happened" (the bulge in birth rates twenty years ago). *The increase in the size of the work-force population is one of the most important domestic facts of life for the next decade. It will create powerful political pressure for economic growth.*

Taxes. Forced to opt for higher tax rates or higher taxable incomes, the government will opt for the latter. This will provide another powerful incentive for economic growth, the best means of generating higher corporate and personal taxable incomes. We would not be surprised if tax *rates* went up a bit, too, following the 1972 election.

The tax structure. The underlying tax structure of the nation is so basic to economic performance and its stability so taken for granted that major alterations could have a profound effect on consumer mood and corporate results. Important changes may take place in this decade. Local and state governments are having difficulty raising new funds; courts are questioning the constitutionality of school taxes; and at the federal level there is talk of "value added" taxes as a replacement for, or supplement to, property taxes. Investors should be on the alert for possible, if not necessarily desirable, change in this area.

The demands for credit. They will continue to be immense in order to help finance economic growth, defense, and social change. Interest rates will be higher, on the average, this decade than last. Common stocks will be more sensitive to interest rate changes.

Unemployment. The high rate of eligible additions to the work force will slow the rate, and the extent, of improvements in unemployment figures. We don't see how the figure can be held much below 5 percent. Unemployment statistics will be revised to determine in greater depth the true degree and composition of unemployment.

Inflation. With unemployment at the 5–5.5 percent level, on the average, we believe inflation can be held to a 3.5 to 4 percent range over the next year or two. Over the long run we are less sanguine. No free industrialized nation has yet solved the problem of achieving both full employment and price stability for very long. The speculative distortions of inflation must continue to be a source of investor concern in the 1970s.

Real growth. Future productivity gains are the key. For the next two to three years, real economic growth may amount to 5 percent or more. Over the longer run we expect real growth to be lower—probably in the 3 to 4 percent range.

Government regulation. Alfred North Whitehead wrote many years ago that "It is idle to suppose that corporations will not be brought more and more under public control." He was right. There will certainly be more supervision: more regulation of product quality, of selling practices, of manufacturing processes, of rates of return; there will be more insistence on full and prompt disclosure of information. We may also see more formal public-private partnerships of the sort typified by Comsat and Fanny May. Whether the growing role of government in business will be handled in a sensible way that protects the legitimate interests of consumers and of society, or whether we all drown in paperwork and bureaucratic confusion, is a major unresolved issue of the decade. The answer depends on the maturity of our corporate leaders and the quality of the public officials we elect.

Social turmoil. There will be less *visible* unrest, less violence, in the first half of the seventies than in the last half of the sixties, not because social problems will have been solved but because expectations may be less utopian. Students and teachers will be more interested in jobs than in issues. So, for better or worse, will most other people.

The International Financial Scene

The multiple realignment of national exchange rates negotiated as part of the Smithsonian settlement in December 1971 has partially cleared the air. By this we mean:

- We are not likely for the next few years to have a major, confidence-jarring international monetary crisis of the sort to which we have so reluctantly become accustomed.
- Foreign investors, who have moved billions of dollars in and out of U.S. markets in recent years (contributing to instability), may find U.S. common stocks more attractive as a result of recent exchange-rate changes and are likely to be net buyers in the period ahead. In the next section of this chapter we talk about the 31 million American owners of U.S. common stocks. One should not forget that there are also, for U.S. equities, growing numbers of European, Japanese, and other foreign investors. Foreign capital markets are still relatively undeveloped. The opportunities for corporations to raise equity capital here—and for investors throughout the world to find equity investments here—are still unmatched elsewhere.
- Despite the many manifestations of resentment at American domination of business abroad, there continues to be a growing commitment by European banking firms to participation in the American new issues and stock markets. Many English, French,

and German banks have joined our regional stock exchanges. A representative of one of the main German banks serves as vice chairman of the Boston Stock Exchange.

• Mounting protectionist pressures have been temporarily checked.

• Opportunities for the growth of American corporations overseas remain relatively promising. The increased costs of overseas investments as a result of exchange realignments are somewhat offset by the improved value of the earnings generated in the revalued currencies.

In addition to the Smithsonian settlement, prospects for more U.S. trade with the Eastern Bloc nations have recently improved. This change is difficult to measure and may in its early stages involve only Western European subsidiaries of American companies (rather than U.S. exports). On balance it is a favorable prospect. (The more exciting possibility of opening major markets in the U.S.S.R. and Red China is further off but could materialize to some extent in this decade.)

Having said this, we should also indicate that there are many fundamental unsolved problems on the international scene. These include the continuing need to develop new reserve assets to finance the growth of the world economy. Will the dollar continue to function as a reserve currency, or has it been sufficiently discredited to create the necessary pressure to replace it with something else? Will that something else be Special Drawing Rights or higher-priced gold? The issue is far from resolved.

What is the financial significance of the United Kingdom's entry into the Common Market? Will this lead to a more powerful, centralized common financial market abroad? If so, what are the implications for our own financial community and investors here?

Recent diplomatic setbacks for the Japanese, and the concomitant loosening of their ties to the United States, will have as yet unknown ramifications with regard to future diplomatic and economic relationships among Japan, China, the United States, and other Far Eastern nations.

There is a fundamental tendency for the United States to run balance-of-payment deficits. In part this results from our commitment to full employment and to a high standard of living. In part, also, it is the inevitable result of our highly developed capital markets; over the long run we are more likely to be an exporter than an importer of most kinds of capital. In our judgment we will not have to wait another forty years for another devaluation.

The Financial Community

The cult of the personality on Wall Street appears to be dead. When we ask our Wall Street friends who is doing a good job managing funds, we aren't given the names of individuals—like Jerry Tsai, Howard Stein, or Roland Grimm, as in the old days—but rather the names of institutions: the T. Rowe Price Group, the people over at Morgan's, or Jennison Associates.

By the end of the 1960s 30 percent of all outstanding common stocks in the country were owned by financial institutions and more than half of all trading in securities was accounted for by these groups. It has been said* that these institutions cannot possibly continue to increase their holdings of stocks at the same rates in the next decade as they did in the last two. And of course they cannot. They are already very large, and their common stock holdings represent a larger percent of total investment than formerly. *But they will grow*—particularly pension funds, as demands for higher and more flexible pension benefits grow.

The size of pension funds, the growing sophistication of pension fund managers, their willingness to move quickly from stock to stock (or from stocks to bonds) to find the highest possible "total return," and the fact that these funds pay no taxes (so there is no pressure to retain securities to avoid capital-gains levies)—these four factors are likely to contribute to market volatility in the years ahead. This means that swings in the prices of many individual

---

* By *Fortune* magazine: "A Bad New Era for Common Stocks," October 1971.

stocks will be faster and wider than before, as well as those in stock and bond prices as a whole.

Now we come to the question of you—the individual investor: up from 20 million a decade ago to your present 31 million. For the four-year period 1967–1970, you sold $35 billion of common stocks and bought $25 billion of corporate bonds! Pension funds exchanged their bonds for your stocks. The exchange may have increased your *immediate* return (bonds providing higher interest rates than common stock dividends), but we wonder how much this shift will really prove over the long run, since *the pension funds, after all, are administered for your benefit.*

When individual investors buy or sell common stocks on a massive scale, confidence is usually involved—confidence (or lack thereof) in the President, in the political system, in the economy, in our ability to solve national problems, or in the integrity and stability of the financial community. In the first chapter of this book we described the events that helped destroy confidence as the 1960s ran their course. So far in this chapter we have given an informal overview of the national and international setting in which investors will be making choices in the period ahead. We would describe that summary as "guardedly optimistic"—a favorite Wall Street phrase.

But what of the Wall Street setting? Is the Street going to settle down? Are the large houses in good financial shape? Are they interested in, and capable of, serving you?

Wall Street is in the throes of a classic American business adjustment. Many small, family-controlled partnerships are being consolidated into a smaller number of professionally managed corporations, some of which have sold shares to the public for the first time. The consolidation has been forced by the mistakes of the past (for some firms it has been a question of merge or perish). It results also from the recognition that new risks and uncertainties—having to do with competition, with pricing, and with regulation—require more varied and able managers. And, finally, there is the urgent need for capital. No longer can the typical Wall

Street firm finance itself by means of customer balances, bank borrowings, and the retained earnings of individual partners. Long in the position of helping other American corporations raise money, the Street must go to the Street for funds itself. While the firms themselves seem traumatized by these developments, there is nothing really very abnormal about this transition if one studies the history of other industries.

If, and when, the dust settles, we believe the changes will prove beneficial for investors—individuals included. The needs of individuals are likely to end up being served by a smaller number of large, strongly financed, well-run, national (and sometimes international) firms. We hope and believe there will be one national security exchange. If these changes materialize, service should be more flexible, more efficient, and more reasonably priced. Furthermore, faced for the first time with the discipline of public ownership (a discipline that will be appropriately intensified by the fact that these firms' owners will also be their customers), the managers of these Wall Street companies will be forced to practice the virtues they have so frequently preached to their corporate clients. They will be forced, in short, to install stringent financial controls, to think hard about manpower development, and to engage in *real* long-range planning. As they do so, they are likely to become more astute and more demanding in their judgments of *other* corporate managements. The gullibility of Wall Street corporate underwriting and research departments—whose facile appraisals of corporate earnings projections have led to the cluttering of the marketplace and your portfolios with untold numbers of third-rate common stocks—may be less pronounced.

That could be one of the best things that ever happened to you.

The Consumer

The American consumer—his income, his moods, his values, his tastes—will do more in a peacetime economy to affect the fortunes of individual companies and investors than anyone else. Last year he spent over $600 billion of the trillion dollars that make up our Gross National Product.

There are an estimated 26.5 million families in the United States (51 percent of the entire population) that make less than $10,000 per year. Most of the new families that join the work force—as mentioned, the largest increment to our population in the coming decade—will first join that group. These families are "on the make," working hard for higher income, security, and mobility. Many of them have working wives. They share a desire to gain a larger share of the national affluence they see around them. They will comprise the largest—and most dynamic—sector of the consumer market in the next decade. They are interested in convenience, in service, in value. They are still interested in "mass" products and services—even though their tastes will become more specialized as they move up the economic ladder.

Within our vast system we believe that those companies that will be the most responsive to the needs of consumers will be moderate-sized corporations, with annual sales of $50 million to $250 million. These companies can innovate more spontaneously and react more effectively to changing times than can the majority of the large corporations. Moderate-sized companies appear to have a freedom and a flexibility to design new products, new services, and new systems, and to adapt more readily to the current constraints being imposed on the corporate world by federal, state, and local regulations. As we observed earlier in this book, the greatest earnings growth and greatest stock price appreciation have been achieved by companies of this sort.

Growth vs. the Quality of Life

Corporations exist to fill needs. In a society as large and diverse as ours, there is an infinite variety of needs to be served—frivolous and essential, simple and complex.

We have just suggested that many investment opportunities will continue to be provided by corporations adroit enough to respond to the material needs of the American consumer. But what of the growing number of voices crying that growth in consumer consumption must be checked? For this is what the proponents of zero economic growth really espouse—a leveling off of aggregate consumption and, thus, output—in order to preserve the environment and the race.

We fully agree that mindless, unplanned growth is dangerous, but stagnation is equally perilous. Zbigniew Brzezinski recently wrote, "That inequality exists in the United States is indisputable. However, what has made inequality bearable is that in the American tradition (as well as myth) it is balanced by opportunity. Opportunity requires flexibility and mobility, and these are created by growth. Growth—through inventiveness, initiative, creativity—makes it possible for an individual to rise or at least entertain the dream of rising."

The issue of growth vs. the quality of life is here to stay. The way in which it is debated and the manner in which various "trade-offs" are resolved will have profound consequences, ultimately, for all of us not only as investors but as citizens and parents as well.

In the 1970s the issues must be resolved not on the basis of a simplistic choice between growth and no growth but rather on purposeful decisions regarding the *nature* and *rate* of economic growth.

Stagnation will be a disaster for investors. So will unplanned growth—although it may take a decade or more for Wall Street to realize it. But in a world in which national goals are established, in which economic growth is more carefully managed to provide a "return on investment" for the community and for succeeding generations as well as for individuals and corporations, all kinds of new opportunities for corporate endeavor will materialize.

Under these hopefully not utopian circumstances, corporations will be increasingly challenged to meet the needs of society as a whole: developing new sources of energy and protein, finding new ways to prevent and cure disease, devising more effective forms of education, providing better shelter and mass transport, and manag-

ing the disposal or recycling of waste materials in ways that en-
courage and preserve the health of our planet.

While the needs served by corporations change, the qualities that
enable business enterprises to meet them do not.

Whether a given corporation is attempting to meet the material
needs of the individual or the more subtle, intangible, precious
needs of the community at large (or perhaps attempting both), innovative spirit and managerial discipline will continue to be the
essential ingredients of success.

Appendix: The Revival of the Long-Term Bond Market

J UST when most investors, private as well as institutional, had sounded the death knell of the bond market, and corporate trustees had authorized vastly increased commitments from the contractual savings of institutions (pension funds) to the equity market, a drastic combination of circumstances, phoenix-like, revived the long-term bond market. The following developments help explain this about-face:

- A shortfall between corporate cash flow and capital spending required increased outside financing by debt during the late 1960s.
- Tight money policies to restrain inflation, coupled with growing credit demands, drove interest rates to the highest levels in more than one hundred years.
- A corporate financial crisis forced companies to rebuild their balance sheets and to restore their liquidity, which they accomplished by the sale of long-term corporate debt to replace short-term bank loans.
- Chronic budget deficits of federal, state, and local governments resulted in increased borrowing by these agencies to finance both current operating needs and long-term projects.

• The federal government expanded its use of off–balance sheet financing of government-sponsored agencies to minimize official budget deficits while increasing spending. The Federal National Mortgage Association and, most recently, the U.S. Postal Service epitomize U.S. activities that have become partially privately owned and which finance through private credit markets.

Credit market financing by nonfinancial corporations rose from an annual average of $10 to $15 billion in the years prior to 1965 to more than $40 billion per year in 1970 and 1971. To make it attractive for creditors to provide such huge sums of money, interest rates went up and up in the years between 1965 and 1969. It was the high yields on bonds of all kinds, government, corporate, and tax-exempt, that brought the public's money out of the mattress (and the stock market). It was the small private investor, and not the supposedly astute professional institutional portfolio manager, who first identified the new opportunities in the bond market.

Attracted by the relative improvement in income over other forms of savings, and equally frightened by the buffeting it had received in the stock market between 1966 and 1969, the public increased its purchases of bonds. In 1969 alone, private investors acquired $26 billion worth of all kinds of bonds (U.S. government, federal agencies, foreign, corporate, state, and local). This was more than 50 percent of the volume of net new bonds of all types that were offered. When the Penn Central bankruptcy catastrophe struck, the public's and institutions' previous concepts of investment safety were shattered. Demand for safety of principal became preeminent. Money was withdrawn from the stock market, from savings banks, from commercial paper—and from stockings —to buy only the highest-grade long-term bonds. Investors had learned the hard way again that inflation was not necessarily good for equities and bad for bonds.

What are the basic characteristics of a bond? And what are the essential features that we look for when investing in a bond? Bonds and preferred stocks are fixed-income securities. The investor expects to receive an unchanging income, without great fluctuations in the value of his principal. Without delving too deeply into the many complexities and subtleties that distinguish various types of fixed-income securities, what are the essential points to consider when buying bonds (or preferred stocks)? The best discussion of the principles of fixed-income selection can be found in Graham, Dodd, and Cottle's *Security Analysis.**

The most important thing you are looking for is *safety*. Can the company that issues the bond or other form of fixed-income security meet its obligations under all conditions? There is a simple quantitative measure of the ability of a company to meet its obligations, that is, the extent to which its earnings before taxes and interest payments meet its annual interest requirements. While that test alone, known as "interest coverage," is important, it is not complete. You must know enough about the company whose bonds you are buying, the nature of its business, its past record, its assets, and its total capitalization to be sure that it can pay off the principal of the debt as well as meet its annual interest rate requirements.

Certain organizations have existed for many years to provide independent assessments of the financial standing of the issues of debt obligations. The two principal rating groups to which the purchasers of fixed-income securities refer are Moody's and Standard & Poor's. Each of these organizations rates potential offerings on a scale from the highest degree of safety to the least protection. A rating by one or both of these groups plays an important role in the relative interest rate that the company will have to pay. The higher the rating on the scale, the lower the interest rate.

In making your investments in fixed-income securities you should always ask your adviser to provide you with these ratings. They will help you to formulate your judgment about the bonds or preferred stocks you are buying. While the rating agencies are not infallible either, their ratings are often the basis for the market's acceptance of a bond, and there is sufficient substance in their

* New York: McGraw-Hill, 1962.

credit judgment for you to count them an important element in your evaluation, but you must also use your own common sense.

In the spring of 1970 New Jersey Bell Telephone offered debentures with an interest rate of 9⅜ percent, which were rated AAA by Moody's and Standard & Poor's. Many lesser-grade issues were forced to pay in excess of 10 percent interest per annum.

In the aftermath of the Penn Central affair, the demand for safety became so elemental that many fine but secondary companies who wanted to raise money by the corporate debt route had to pay excessively high interest rates.

The availability of billions of dollars of bonds with such returns, combined with rising investor demand, improved the liquidity of the bond market. Markets for these bonds improved not only on the listed exchanges but in the over-the-counter markets made by firms such as Salomon Brothers and Goldman, Sachs.

The comparative returns available from corporate bonds, combined with increased volume, choice, and marketability, belatedly brought institutional investors back into the bond market. The institutional investor recognized what the private investor had instinctively understood—that when bond yields were comparable to the "long-term rate of return of equities," bonds must be purchased. This shift in view shattered the investment philosophies of many long-term 100-percent-equity believers. Gradually these investors discarded long-standing prejudices against bonds and adapted to the new investment environment.

The anticipation of declining interest rates also suggested the possibility of capital gains (as interest rates go down, bond prices go up) which increase the potential return available to fixed-income investors.

Henry Kaufman, Salomon Brothers' partner and economist, pointed out, in a talk delivered on November 24, 1971, entitled "The Bond and Stock Markets in Phase II," that "since the start of 1968 through October 1971, the simple rate of return on newly offered high-grade corporate bonds measured by the annual price change plus interest payments, was 19 percent as compared to 12 percent for stocks, measured by the annual change of the Standard & Poor's 500 plus the dividend payments. Since the start of 1970 to October 1971 the rate of return on bonds has been 33 percent versus 9 percent for stocks."*

One response to the burgeoning interest in bonds has been the proliferation of fixed-income mutual funds managed by insurance companies, and mutual funds offering investors safety, diversification and high income.

The experience of the recent past cannot be automatically projected into the future. The extreme fluctuations of long- and short-term interest rates that we experienced between 1966 and 1971, and the turbulent conditions that accompanied and contributed to these extraordinary peaks and valleys, make a repeat of such unusual bond investment opportunities unlikely soon again. Nevertheless, the comparatively high returns still available on some bonds, and the credit demands still anticipated by industry, continue to make bonds a valid investment consideration.

The increased size and scope of bond market offerings gives you, the investor, all kinds of choices. The direction of interest rates will, of course, be the governing factor in your consideration. You can make investments in discount bonds (selling at prices less than the price at which they will ultimately be redeemed), with a sure long-term capital gain built in on top of a good current return. You can invest at good current returns in bonds that offer a high current income but a modest potential capital loss because the recent decrease in interest rates has increased their market price to a premium over the price at which they will be called or redeemed at maturity. You can move freely between alternatives to meet your changing investment needs.

Much more could be said about the complexities of bond markets, whose total dollar size dwarfs that of the equity market.

* This result can change substantially and rapidly. A subsequent study by Dr. Kaufman showed after the stock market recovery at year end 1971 that from the price lows of 1970 to year end 1971, however, stocks have shown a total return of 54 percent as compared with 39 percent, the best bond return.

The growing interest in bonds has come about in an environment of declining interest rates, weak economic activity, and efforts to restrain inflation. What will happen to the bond market if these forces are reversed? Will the liquidity and flexibility of recent days still be there? We don't know. Our point in this book, which emphasizes the opportunities that still exist in the stock market, is to recognize the reemergence of bonds as an appropriate investment alternative, to be considered when they offer a return commensurate with the overall return on capital you are seeking.

Index

72 73 74 75 10 9 8 7 6 5 4 3 2 1